EXPERIENCE ALASKA

A TOURIST'S GUIDE TO ALASKA: NORTH TO THE
FUTURE, THE LAST FRONTIER

LM TAYLOR

CONTENTS

Part II
REGIONS OF ALASKA

INTRODUCTION

If you are looking for your next extended vacation destination where you can enjoy nature, see breathtaking landscapes, and meet friendly locals, the search is over. Alaska is the destination you are looking for. With thousands of miles of beautiful coastline, ancient glaciers, majestic mountain ranges, and untouched forests, the scenery is like no other. You can see wildlife up close, fish for fresh salmon and halibut, sample local craft beers, engage in all manner of outdoor sports, enjoy the freshest seafood, and witness the grandeur of the northern lights. Can you imagine any other place where all this is possible?

Known as the Last Frontier, the largest state in the United States is a unique opportunity to learn about different cultures, explore and discover places not yet touched by man, and visit one of its *eight* national parks, a number rivaled only by California, with one more. According to *5 Reasons Why Alaska Should be on Your Travel List* (2023), these national parks are home to 98% of the bear population in the U.S. (100,000), caribou (9,000,000), mountain goats, wolves, bison and musk ox just to name a few. Not to mention all the marine life that calls the Alaskan wilderness home, including humpback whales, orcas, puffins, salmon sharks, sea otters, and sea lions.

Imagine kayaking between glaciers, catching a helicopter to the top of a snowy mountain, hiking pristine wilderness trails, or simply admiring some of the highest peaks in the world from a safer venue. Fishing, hiking, mountain climbing, white water rafting, ice-climbing, skiing, snowboarding, and even boating just to admire the area are just a few of the activities that draw people from all over the world to Alaska. And for those who prefer to observe from a more comfortable vantage point, ample opportunity exists to ride a helicopter or small plane in order to admire the panoramic view from above. You can even land on a glacier!

While all this nature is incredible, it is impossible to forget the welcoming and warm locals, who receive tourists as if they were next-door neighbors they have known their entire lives. There is so much cultural diversity to be amazed by, including many towns built during the gold rush, fishing villages on the coast, and other smaller locations with only a few inhabitants. In these towns, you can experience their incredible traditions and local delicacies and be amazed at their reverence for the land.

With so much to do and offer, Alaska is perfect for a week-long stay or even longer. Because there is plenty to do, the longer you stay, the more enchanted you will become with everything around you. If you are looking for a different experience away from the crowds that attract many tourists, and one that offers plenty of contact with nature, this is undoubtedly the place to go.

However, it is understandable if you are reluctant to start planning just yet with so little information on the destination. More frequently than not, travel books to the region offer the same experiences that lack the connection and emotion you look for when visiting such a unique place. This will give you all the necessary information to have the best travel experience possible while providing all the information required to explore on your own.

Throughout the next 10 chapters, we will explore all the different things you should consider, ranging from what items to take to the best options for travel and logistics. As you start each chapter, you will learn more about Alaska's regions, history, local culture, traditions, tips on the best adventures, and places to watch wildlife. Finally, as we are talking about a place with some remote and difficult-to-access regions, we will talk about safety and best practices to ensure you have a safe and unforgettable vacation.

If you are ready to embark on a journey to discover Alaska's natural beauty, diverse attractions, and unique experiences, read on! Once you are done, you will understand why the state is becoming a favorite destination for travelers seeking adventure, relaxation, and a chance to connect with nature. Grab your coat and hiking boots without further delay, and let's get ready to discover the Last Frontier.

PART I
INTRODUCTION TO ALASKA

AN ALASKAN ADVENTURE

> *Alaska has long been a magnet for dreamers and misfits, people who think the unsullied enormity of the Last Frontier will patch all the holes in their lives. The bush is an unforgiving place, however, that cares nothing for hope or longing.*

— JON KRAKAUER

Understanding a new destination's history and the cultural roots of the people who live there is essential when visiting. This is no different for those who want to visit Alaska. Although it is currently one of the 50 American states, this was not always the case. In fact, Alaska belonged to Russia in the 18th century before becoming part of the U.S. territory.

In this first chapter, we will explore Alaska's essence, understanding the symbolism behind its nickname, "the Last Frontier," and its state motto, "North to the Future." As we do this, we will unravel the fascinating tapestry of its history and cultural significance.

THE LAST FRONTIER

Usually referred to as "The Last Frontier," the nickname of the 49th state originates from the amount of unexplored and unsettled land. The state's name is derived "from the Aleut *alaxsxaq*, meaning 'the mainland' or, more literally, *the* 'object towards which the action of the sea is directed.' It is also known as *Alyeska*, the 'great land,' an Aleut word derived from the same root" (*Alaska Kids' Corner*, n.d.).

The state's motto, "North to the Future," was created in 1967 when it celebrated its 100-year purchase from Russia. This motto's main idea is that Alaska is the land of promise and the unexpected, which you will soon learn fits this state perfectly.

As you will explore later in this chapter and book, Alaska is divided into five regions. Its capital, Juneau, is located in the southeast region and has an approximate population of 33,000 (*Alaska Kids' Corner*, n.d.). The other regions are the Arctic, Interior, Southcentral, and Southwest.

Alaska has been through many colonization attempts and has had influence from other cultures throughout its development and occupation. From Russians to Spanish and Americans, the promise of gold, oil, and other riches attracted thousands of travelers who wanted to find wealth by exploring the region. Nonetheless, its primary occupants, the Eskimos, remained a fishing community. This activity continues to be explored today and is culturally significant to its people.

BRIEF HISTORY OF ALASKA

To understand the impact of different cultures on the state's inhabitants, it is important to understand its history. For a land that was previously occupied by dinosaurs and other animals and only welcomed the first humans through the Bering Land Bridge more than 20,000 years ago, Alaska has a rich and diverse history that should be shared. Read on to learn more about what makes Alaskan culture so unique and the different occupations it has faced throughout the centuries.

Pre-Colonial Inhabitants

Different migrant groups used the Bering Land Bridge to move from Siberia into Alaska. These populations usually followed the animals they were hunting or herding in the quest for food. While the first of these groups did not stay in the region, the land that would eventually become Alaska started having its first settlers 10,000 years after the arrival of the first humans. Among these were the Inuit, Haida, and Tlingit people who arrived and established themselves in the region (Lynch & Miller, 2019).

Russian Colonization

By the mid-1700s, with the discovery of "new land" east of Russian territory, explorers started to settle in the region, which became popular for the commerce of animal fur. Nevertheless, the local population was not happy with the new colonizers and would fight them off at every new attempt at establishment. To ensure that the Natives would be more receptive to them, marriages between Russian men and local tribal women became the norm in the region.

This led to a more extensive integration and the settlement of Russians in the region. The locals would often be pressured to change religions and traditions. By then, the United States had entered an agreement with the Russians, and from 1824 to 1867, the region was controlled by what was known as the Russian–American Company. The exhaustive exploration of sea lions almost led to their extinction in the area. The wars in Russia soon became a reason for Russia to accept selling the territory to the Americans, which happened in 1867 (Lynch & Miller, 2019).

U.S. Purchase and the Gold Rush

In 1867, the United States purchased Alaska from Russia for $7.2 million, a move initially criticized since many Americans did not see the advantage of having the territory as a part of the country. Nonetheless, different missionaries started migrating to the area to spread American culture. Almost 100 years after its purchase, in 1959, Alaska was finally recognized as an American state by President Eisenhower (History.com, 2022).

During this time, Russians and Americans did not widely know that gold had been found in the region as early as 1861. Throughout the subsequent years, the spread of this information attracted more people to explore Alaska. Between 1897 and 1900, the number of explorers and miners who wanted a chance to strike it rich by finding gold grew exponentially, leading to the establishment of other cities by Americans and Canadians. "The Klondike Gold Rush brought more than 100,000 prospectors to Alaska, including author and journalist Jack London. It led to more than 50 gold-mining camps over the next decade" (History.com, 2022).

World War II

During World War II, Alaska became a territory of dispute when the Japanese invaded three islands and wanted to control the region. My grandfather was actually a radar operator on a U.S. Navy Destroyer, the USS Gillespie, which participated patrolling the Aleutian Islands, as well bombarding the island of Attu during the Japanese occupation in January - March 1943. Many Americans were not even aware that this portion of U.S. soil was occupied during World War II until years laters, but that is a story for another book.

Due to this occupation, the government decided to develop the area and build airports and military bases to protect the territory. The U.S. Army was responsible for removing "most of the Unangan from the Aleutian Islands and sending them to work in canneries, sawmills, hospitals, and schools or to internment camps in Juneau or on the southeastern islands. Disease—particularly influenza and tuberculosis—killed many Unangan during this period" (Lynch & Miller, 2019).

Once the war ended, a referendum was held, and the Americans voted to transform the territory into the 49th state. With a favorable result, Alaska was incorporated in 1959 and has since been important to the country, especially with the discovery of oil and gas in the 1950s. Despite current environmental concerns and governmental suspensions and permits regarding pipelines and gas exploration in the region, it remains an important center for the country for oil and gas and as a military region.

CULTURAL HERITAGE AND SIGNIFICANCE

With its extensive history and the maintenance of traditional cultural aspects from its first inhabitants, Alaska's culture is one of many attractions for visitors. Today, many indigenous cultures remain and are a part of the state's identity, including incorporating words into the local vocabulary and naming natural resources. "About 15% of Alaska's 730,000 residents are Alaska Native, with 20 distinct cultures and 300 different dialects" (*Alaska Native Culture*, n.d.).

Today, many of the Native people of Alaska live along the coastline, relying on hunting, fishing, and tourism to survive.

Visitors who travel to the state will be able to see the impact and the history of the constructions and villages as they travel. These include Russian Orthodox churches, tribal art and totem poles, the railroads from the Gold Rush era, and even the sled races with trained dogs. These are all part of the state's history, which delight those who chose to immerse themselves in the Alaskan culture.

Cuisine

Alaska's cuisine is primarily based on seafood, mainly due to the volume of salmon captured in the sea and rivers annually. But there is much more to its cuisine than just salmon, and during your visit, you will be able to taste local delicacies that are not found anywhere else. These include reindeer sausages, ice cream made with animal fats and fruits (known as *akutaq*), caribou and moose meat, and some of its incredible local artisan beers.

It is common for much of the food to be homemade and for many families to have their own recipes. Since food can be scarce during the winter, many families stock their fridges with fatty and high-calorie products to help them stay full and fight the cold. Today, although many larger towns have popular restaurant chains and common dishes, there is still the possibility of tasting more local flavors in smaller towns and even trying the original *akutaq* recipe if you meet the right locals.

Cultural Events

Visiting Alaska also means visitors can experience important cultural events celebrating their heritage. Most of these events are held from late February to early November. From the traditional sled races to ice sculpture and Native arts festivals, there are many options to choose from. Although many events are held state-wide, some towns will have specific festivals and celebrations that are the perfect opportunity to meet locals and learn about their culture.

Finally, during the summer, when there is the possibility of enjoying 24 straight hours of sunlight, the most popular events happen, such as fairs and competitions. Known as the period for the "midnight sun," this is certainly not the time to go if you intend to see the northern lights. In fact, the amount of daylight is one of the main challenges for tourists visiting during this time.

If you intend to visit the state to see the aurora borealis or the northern lights, your choice should be to go between August and April, when the dark sky will make them even more visible. At this time of the year, contrary to what happens in the summer, the nights are longer, and sometimes there is no sunlight at all. You also want to plan to see the lights in a remote area since city lights can interfere with how intensely you can see them. Visiting natural hot springs located farther north in the state are a tourist favorite for this activity.

"Northern lights tours are available in the Interior, Arctic, and Southcentral regions. Tour guides know the best spots for viewing and can take you off the beaten track to remote viewing locations with less ambient light" (*Northern Lights*, n.d.). If you are confused about how to best experience each region and what you will see on your trip, don't worry! As you move on to the next section, you will have a brief overview of each of the state's regions, and each of the following chapters of this book will be dedicated to one as well.

Are you ready to start planning?

ALASKA'S FIVE REGIONS

Due to its vast territory, Alaska is divided into five regions, each with distinctive characteristics that make it unique. From the Arctic in the extreme north of the state to the more highly populated Southcentral, each region has something for visitors. As mentioned above, each chapter of this book will be dedicated to a region and cover what you won't want to miss. This will help you choose the one (or ones) to visit that you find the most interesting and exciting.

The five regions are

1. **Arctic:** The state's most remote and unexplored region, inside the Arctic Circle and the coldest regions. Nonetheless, the opportunities to engage with smaller communities that you will see in Chapter 10 are the perfect opportunity for cultural immersion.
2. **Inside Passage (Southeast):** Home to most of the state's glaciers, this is the place to go for magnificent Pacific scenery and wildlife watching, which you will learn more about in Chapter 8.
3. **Interior:** This region has inland wildlife, including bears, moose, caribou, wolves, and different birds. Because of its mountains and tundras, it is a perfect

place to integrate with nature and see some of America's tallest peaks, which will be explored in Chapter 9.

4. **Southcentral:** Home to most of the Alaskan population, the most developed towns, including the state's most populated city, Anchorage, are located here. You will be able to explore this region more in Chapter 6.

5. **Southwest:** With a similar wildlife and landscape to the interior, this region will be explored in Chapter 7. It offers fantastic opportunities to see the coastline, engage in adventures, and explore magnificent sceneries that will surely be unforgettable.

As you continue to explore the preparations needed for your Alaska trip, one decision you need to make is how you will get there and move around once you arrive. In the next section, you will learn all about the best ways to get around the state and what you should keep in mind when doing so. From major airports to highways and railroads, every possibility will be covered to help you plan how you will get around during your visit.

GETTING THERE—
TRANSPORTATION TO AND
AROUND ALASKA

66 *When you travel in Alaska you are humbled by its size and wildness, awed by its beauty, inspired by its original peoples whose culture is still deeply rooted.*

— DAVID ROBERTS

Many traveling to Alaska are usually still determining the best ways to reach the state or how to get around once they are there. Figuring this out is one of the keys to a successful journey. In this chapter, you will see many different options to get there, including by air, land, and water, all of which will allow you to enjoy the magnificent scenery the state offers.

This chapter will provide indispensable insights, tips, and considerations for every mode of travel, from flying into major airports to riding the iconic Alaska Railroad, cruising the marine highways, exploring in an R.V., and navigating local transportation.

FLYING INTO ALASKA

When flying into Alaska, there are several airport options, especially in the main cities of Anchorage, Fairbanks, and Juneau. Major American airlines, such as American Airlines, Delta Airlines, and United Airlines, and others, such as Alaska Airlines, have nonstop routes from major American cities to the state. If you live in Canada, it is possible to find a flight from Air Canada leaving from Vancouver; in the summer, Air Canada to Alaska departs from Frankfurt, Germany.

If you are not going to any of these three cities, you will likely still need to land in one of their airports since they are also hubs that connect to the smaller and local airports in the state. In order of size, the Anchorage airport is the largest one that receives the greatest number of flights, followed by Fairbanks and Juneau. One of the things you will notice in many of these airports is the welcoming atmosphere, and you will even see several taxidermized animals that call the state home up close as you walk by. If you want to rent a car for your visit, you can do that at any of these airports.

Nonetheless, depending on where you plan to visit and the regions you want to explore, you might want to find a closer airport so that you do not have to make as many connections. This will help you save time and resources, making your trip more budget-friendly. There are also a few other tips that you might want to consider to save some money on flights, which can be rather costly during summer, the state's peak season.

Since these are the least sought-after flights, the prices for the red-eye and flights on Tuesdays and Thursdays will be lower than those on weekends or Fridays. Additionally, if you already know when you will be traveling, buying the tickets as early as possible will help you save some cash. Being flexible on the dates is also important, especially for trips during the peak season. To receive the best offers and prices, you might want to set up an alert on your preferred flight tracker app to be notified of a sale or a price drop.

Another thing you might want to consider is not getting attached to "round-trip ticket purchases with one airline or to and from one Alaska destination. Sometimes buying two one-way tickets from different airlines can save costs and offer the in-state travel flexibility of arriving and departing from different Alaska airports" (Annie, 2020). If cost is a concern for you, you might also want to consider having a layover or booking flights with more connections, which tends to make the cost cheaper. Finally, you might want to consider using your credit card miles and airline fidelity cards to reduce costs or even have benefits in luggage dispatch.

According to *Getting to and Around Alaska* (n.d.), the average time it takes to fly between airports in Alaska is the following:

- Anchorage to Fairbanks: 50 minutes
- Anchorage to Juneau: 1.5 hours
- Anchorage to Kenai: 30 minutes
- Anchorage to Nome: 1.5 hours
- Anchorage to Utqiaġvik (Barrow): 2 hours

- Fairbanks to Deadhorse/Prudhoe Bay: 1 hour
- Juneau to Ketchikan: 1 hour
- Juneau to Sitka: 45 minutes

Finally, suppose your main goal during your visit to Alaska is to see one of its national parks. In that case, you might be interested in learning about the airports closest to them. They are the following:

- Denali National Park: Fairbanks Airport
- Glacier Bay National Park: Gustavus Airport
- Katmai National Park: King Salmon Airport
- Kenai Fjords National Park: Ted Stevens Anchorage International Airport
- Klondike Gold Rush National Historical Park: Skagway Airport
- Kobuk Valley National Park: Ralph Wien Memorial Airport
- Sitka National Historical Park: Sitka Airport
- Wrangell-St. Elias National Park and Preserve: Ted Stevens Anchorage International Airport

Once you arrive in Alaska, there are several opportunities to explore. Locally, the state has several options for visitors to get around, from the Alaska Railroad to marine highways and roads. As we explore the options you will have once you land, it is important to consider the weather conditions when you visit and take all the necessary precautions to ensure a safe trip.

The first option we will explore is the Alaska Railroad, one of the prime options for those who want to enjoy the beautiful landscape without having the drive themselves, and it even connects between the state's most important airports.

ALASKA RAILROAD

The Alaska Railroad is an incredible opportunity for those who want to enjoy a cross-state trip without driving. Crossing Alaska from the north, in Fairbanks, to the south, in Seward, with a length of approximately 470 miles, visitors can select from one of the five routes available:

- **Aurora Winter:** This seasonal train operates only through fall to early spring and connects Anchorage to Fairbanks, with stops in Talkeetna and Hurricane. Trains depart from either location approximately every hour, and it takes about 8 hours to get from one end to the other.
- **Coastal Classic:** This train is used to travel between Seward and Anchorage, and it has one stop in Girdwood. It takes approximately 4 hours and can be done as a day trip to visit one end or the other. Throughout the trip, it is possible to see glaciers, waterfalls, wildlife, and other beautiful sights.
- **Denali Star:** This is the main route offered by the Alaska Railroad, connecting Anchorage to Fairbanks, taking about 12 hours. The routes can vary from Anchorage to Denali (8 hours) or Denali to Fairbanks (4 hours), with four companies to choose from. Additional stops include Wasilla and Talkeetna.

Throughout the trip, if the weather allows, seeing the Denali mountain from afar will be possible, granting incredible views of the local landscape.

- **Glacier Discovery:** As the name suggests, this train route is a fantastic opportunity for visitors to travel amid glaciers between Anchorage and Grandview. Some of the stops on the route include Girdwood, Whittier, Portage, and Spencer, and can be completed in approximately 4 hours. Visitors who take this train can enjoy other adventures and experiences if they decide to get off in one of the cities where it stops.
- **Hurricane Turn:** This train makes the short trip between Talkeetna and Hurricane, which takes approximately 2 hours. Locals usually take this route, so if you are looking to meet some residents, this is one of the opportunities to do that. The train departs every 30 minutes and has a different schedule for winter and summer. Since the train goes through the backcountry, you will want to keep your eyes open for the region's bears, wolves, and other wildlife.

Traveling by train is popular in Alaska, especially when the weather is less suitable for driving. Tickets can be bought at the station or online. Still, it is important to consider that there might not be enough room if you wait until the last minute, especially during peak season.

If you want an additional experience on the train, it is possible to book a glass-dome car for some of the routes, which has a glass ceiling so you can enjoy the view even more. In most cases, staying in these cars will be more expensive. "For Adventure Class passengers, there are vista dome cars on the Coastal Classic, Denali Star, and Hurricane Turn Trains. The upper-level seating in the vista domes is unassigned and is open to all passengers on the train" (*When Traveling*, n.d.).

ALASKA MARINE HIGHWAY - FERRIES

If you want to explore Alaska's Southcentral region, the Alaska Marine Highway can be an option. In this state-owned ferry system, it will be possible to navigate not only through the Southcentral coast but also the Inside Passage, the eastern Aleutian Islands, and even British Columbia in Canada. The main objective of this highway is to connect the regions with no accessible driving options. Passengers can embark in the first terminal in Bellingham and leave on the last port in Dutch Harbor in a trajectory that covers over 3,500 miles and has more than 35 stops.

If you take this route and it requires an overnight stay, it is possible to book private cabins to rest in and rely on the diner and restaurant onboard. In addition, if all the suites are booked, "travelers can also sleep in tents and sleeping bags in public areas, including lounges and outdoor solariums. Dining rooms and cafeterias offer hot and cold food for purchase" (*Getting to & Around Alaska by Ferry*, n.d.).

Additionally, while using the ferry as a hop-on, hop-off service is possible, it is important to consider ticket prices since they can be expensive. If you are not traveling by car or by air, you can use the service since the ferries also take walk-in passengers. During the trip, you can view the landscape from the open deck as you go by and take in the beautiful scenery from the water. Some of the most popular routes include: Gulf Coast, Inside Passage, Southcentral Coast, and the Aleutian Islands.

Be sure to arrive early (the recommended time is at least two hours) from departure to guarantee you are well-accommodated, especially for the longer routes. This rule is especially true for those bringing extra equipment or boarding with a car. R.V.s are accepted on the ferries, although you will have to pay extra. Pets are also allowed on some ferries, but they are subject to special conditions, including entrance restrictions, and they need to be kept on a leash.

Remember that if you are traveling by ferry, expect changes to the schedule or delays. It is recommended that there be at least a 30-minute margin for booking flights or trains. Since these ferries can also be relatively full, you may want to bring snacks to avoid lines, expensive food, and long waiting times, especially if you are traveling with children.

Finally, regardless of whether you are traveling with kids or not, it is important to be mindful of a few things to ensure the best experience. These include:

- Keep your belongings near you or locked inside the car at all times.
- Keep children and pets nearby and do not allow them to wander on their own inside the ferry.
- If you are embarking with a car that has an alarm, make sure to turn the alarm off.

- Dress in multiple layers to protect you from the wind and the cold from the water if you want to venture onto the deck.
- Bring hygiene products (including toilet paper or wipes) for the ferry bathroom.
- Remember to pack a few things to keep you entertained, such as games, cards, and even a computer or iPad with your favorite movies and shows already downloaded.
- If the ride is long, ensure your electronics are fully charged and you may want a few pack power banks in case you need to recharge them. Although there are outlets on the ferry, not all of them work properly and many people will likely want to use them.

If you are traveling by car and want to explore the more remote cities, check the road conditions first and see if it is possible to reach them. While many of the cities close to the harbor will have accessible routes, if you are planning to explore inland, this might not necessarily be the case. Be sure to have a backup map in case the GPS fails and you have the necessary internet connection in emergencies.

ALASKA MARINE CRUISES

Another form of transportation that has become very popular in Alaska in the last decade or so are marine cruises. Marine cruises cover a wider area with fewer stops than the ferries, but they of course offer more luxurious accommodations and entertainment. While the vessels still run through the Alaska Marine Highway, they travel a little further away from the coast so that visitors get to explore and see wildlife. In fact, on many of these cruises, the captain will take those onboard to see whales, seals, and other animals that live in the region, as well as glaciers and other remote areas only otherwise accessible by air.

The shorter cruises usually take four to eight hours and will explore a specific region with a round trip. In other cases, it is possible to take a longer route and spend up to a few days on board exploring different areas and stopping at different ports of call. On the longer cruises, many offer private rooms and a full vessel experience to accommodate passengers. However, this will come at a higher price. Depending on the length of the cruise, starting prices can range between $100 to $200 for adults and $50 to $100 for children when they are allowed onboard.

There are two options for those interested in seeing Alaska by cruise: The first is to fly into Alaska and catch the cruise from one of the departing cities. The other is to leave on a cruise from cities like Vancouver or Seattle, where you will go up to Alaska and be brought back. Doing so might save some cash but you will be less likely to visit the inner and rural parts of the state. In addition, it is essential to consider that "restaurant prices in Alaska can be high, but a cruise bundles meals, accommodations, and transportation into one price that, with sales, can be cheaper than you'd think" (Silverstein, 2023).

Some of the most popular routes include exploring the Inside Passage and the Cross Gulf of Alaska, where you will navigate between the glaciers and depart from Seattle or Vancouver. Silverstein (2023) mentions that since many of the cruises in Alaska do not show its beautiful interior, many companies have created the option of a "cruisetour," where they will combine the sailing experience with an inland one on a bus. To some, this will be the ideal option to unite both worlds of exploring by sea and by land.

If you are traveling with children, there are specialized cruises that you might want to consider. In this case, you might want to select one of the cruises with Disney characters and princesses; others have specific areas for children with activities and even the opportunity to meet other kid-beloved characters. Many of these options will also come with opportunities for adults to engage in adventurous activities and enjoy fine dining on board. If you go this route, regardless of your choice, you are certain to have an incredible trip and the time of your life!

DRIVING IN ALASKA

Many people who visit Alaska are usually concerned about driving in the region. It could be because they are afraid of the ice and have no experience, or they may be concerned that the conditions of the roads might not be the best during winter. Granted, it becomes harder to drive when it gets colder and starts to snow. Still, even during the snow and ice season, drivers usually only have a few issues with driving around the main roads. Usually, the main highways have snow removed for traffic.

At the same time, other highways, such as the Denali Park Highway and the Top of the World Highway, are not. In this case, visitors are advised not to drive through them because of the chance of getting stuck and the lack of assistance. Cell phone service can be unstable in some regions, so you may be unable to call for help. Even if you are traveling on roads that have been maintained, you should take a few precautions to ensure that you do not have any accidents.

The main advice when driving in icy or snowy conditions is to slow down. Rushing can be dangerous, especially considering the slippery road and the possibility of animals crossing it. Although fewer cars are on the roads during the winter, "conditions can be icy and snowy along the route, especially in the Yukon and Interior Alaska. Be sure to give yourself extra time for weather and icy road conditions. Studded tires are recommended, and winter tires are required" (*Getting to & Around Alaska: Drive*, n.d.).

You also want to always fill the gas tank whenever possible. Some stations might be closed during the winter, meaning there will be a longer distance between those that are open. Therefore, whenever you can, you should fill up on gas and supplies in case you get stuck somewhere or must take a detour. If you run across a snow removal operation, remember to give the plows enough space, with the recommended distance at least 200 feet.

If you want to use your visit to Alaska to enjoy the scenery through a car window, allowing you more time to explore and stop at the places you find interesting, then driving is good option to consider. As we continue to explore the different options for moving around the state, a few popular routes offer a scenic experience that will make your road trip more than a simple ride. It will be an adventure that you will never forget!

Popular Routes

If you plan on driving to Alaska or renting a car once you are there, you can enjoy some of the best scenery in the world. There is so much that cannot be seen from the water. The Milepost Guide is an excellent resource if you plan on driving to Alaska. However, this does not mean that there aren't challenges. As discussed earlier, several roads are closed from late fall to mid-spring, which means that you might have some challenges getting around, depending on where you are going. Nonetheless, the state offers a website (511.alaska.gov) with extensive information on road closures that can be accessed before your trip. Here are some roads you might want to explore once you reach the state:

Alaska Highway

This is the main highway in Alaska, connecting it to the lower 48 states and British Columbia. It has an extension of approximately 1,400 miles and is open throughout the year. The highway is well-serviced, and there are plenty of gas stations and restaurants throughout the route where travelers can stop for a rest. While the service on the road is mostly good, cell phone service can be spotty in some areas.

George Parks Highway

This road extends approximately 360 miles and connects Fairbanks to Anchorage, making it an ideal route to reach Denali National Park. The trip will award you with incredible vistas of the mountains and parks surrounding the region, with several options to stop and enjoy the region as you drive by.

Glacier Highway

This highway extends for approximately 35 miles and connects most of the cities located within the Inside Passage region of Alaska. Apart from this highway, you will need to use the Alaska Marine Highway Ferry to reach the other islands and areas of the region. However, one of the main attractions of this road is the possibility of seeing dozens of glaciers as you drive, offering several stops for that perfect picture.

North-Council Road

This small road is located in the Arctic part of Alaska, extends for almost 75 miles, and connects the cities of Nome and Council in the north. This road is not only unpaved but also part of the historic gold rush in the state, which today can only be reached by sea, plane, or dogsled. As you might imagine, it is hard to get to despite offering visitors amazing views. Still, there are several ghost villages and structures you will be able to see along the way. Due to the difficulty of accessing it, it is needless to say that this road is usually closed during the winter when there is no maintenance.

Seward Highway

The second most popular highway in the state, the Seward Highway, connects Seward to Anchorage and offers access to some of the most populated cities in the state. It is open throughout the year with an extension of approximately 130 miles. It will take you to some inland locations, with special stops to admire the local scenery. Due to its frequent use and purpose of connecting the southern regions, the highway is open throughout the year. It is worth noting that this highway also includes access to Kenai Fjords National Park. However, you should check the National Park Service (NPS) page to use the inner roads of the park.

Top of the World Highway

This highway's name should indicate what to expect from it: It is the ideal choice if you want to travel to less busy areas and avoid encountering other people. Throughout its 185 miles that extend from Dawson City to Tok, it is one of the most isolated highways in the state. With the exception of Chicken, there are very few stops throughout its extension. If you plan to take this road, you will certainly be able to explore magnificent landscapes. Still, because of its lack of stops, you want to bring everything you might need with you in case of any problems. Due to its isolated nature, if you need help it might take a while to get there.

Mileage and Average Road Time

If you plan to visit by car, it can be helpful to know the distances between the main cities in the state. To help you with this, here is a table showing the mileage between Anchorage and some of the most significant regions. Remember that the average travel time will depend on weather and traffic conditions, so it can be longer, especially in challenging weather conditions.

Route	Average time	Distance
Anchorage to Denali	Between 4 to 5 hours	265 miles
Anchorage to Fairbanks	Between 7 to 8 hours	360 miles
Anchorage to Homer	Between 5 to 6 hours	220 miles
Anchorage to Seward	Between 2 to 3 hours	130 miles
Anchorage to Whittier	Between 1 to 2 hours	65 miles

Tips for Traveling by Car

Those planning to drive through Alaska to explore the state should remember to take some precautions. Whether you are driving your car or renting one, the first thing you should do is make sure the vehicle is suitable for Alaskan conditions and that you have the necessary equipment in case of emergencies. Remember to check the insurance policy and everything it covers if you are using a rental car. Sometimes, the insurance company will not be liable for accidents if the safety recommendations are not followed.

If you are traveling with your car, remember to ensure it is well-maintained and has the necessary elements for a safe trip. This includes checking the brakes and other components that can be "challenged" in colder weather. Cars in Alaska all need a block heater if you are going to park outside in the cold. Remember to always stop, fill up on gas, and restock your supplies wherever possible. Although emergency services are accessible from most areas and tow trucks are available to help drivers, depending on the weather conditions, they might take longer to arrive.

Here are a few additional tips you might want to consider if you are driving through the state:

- Wear layers and comfortable and loose-fit clothing.
- Respect the speed limit.
- Keep your headlights on at all times.
- Beware of wildlife crossing the roads.
- Use the pull-over stops and camping sites along the road if needed.
- Take enough water with you if you get delayed somewhere.
- If traveling through rural or more remote areas, ensure you do not travel alone.
- Have a plan for emergencies.
- If you are renting a car, make sure you reserve it in advance.
- Fill the tank as frequently as possible.
- Check for the spare tire.
- If the weather is not good, take it slow and be patient.
- During the summer, the highways can be rather busy, with long lines waiting to pass slower vehicles. If this is the case, you should not attempt to pass unless it is completely safe.

If you follow all of these safety guidelines, you will enjoy a safe trip! However, remember that exploring the state by car is not the only option. Those interested in saving money can also opt for R.V. rentals and camping since there are many sites for this purpose. Of course, camping is only a viable option when the weather is decent since campsites are susceptible to snow and freezing temperatures at night.

R.V. AND CAMPING

R.V.s and camping are options for those who want to explore Alaska more adventurously. In fact, the activity is so popular among visitors that there are over 30 companies that rent equipment and vehicles for this purpose. Due to the incredible number of people traveling to the state to do this, an association was created to offer those interested the best experience possible. In several areas, you can find private and government-owned R.V. parks, campgrounds, and all the necessary resources to make your trip the best possible.

As you look around online, read testimonials from people who have engaged in the adventure and their recommendations for companies to use. In many cases, these companies will rent camping gear to those interested in exploring independently. In addition to this, according to *Alaska R.V., Motorhome and Campervan Rental* (n.d.), "renting is a pretty cost-effective way to see Alaska. A 14-day R.V. trip in Alaska typically costs less than trips involving airfares, car rentals, hotels, and restaurants."

The added bonus of traveling in an R.V. and camping is that you will have freedom and not necessarily rely on needing to find accommodations wherever you go. There are necessary services in many camping and R.V. sites like showers, dumping, and sometimes even places where you can stock up on supplies. Apart from this, the precautions you will want to take are the same as if driving for a road trip, such as paying attention to the speed limits and filling up the gas tank when possible.

While traveling by car and camping or driving an R.V. is an incredible experience, when considering transportation in Alaska, we could not leave out one of the most traditional forms of moving around in the state: bush planes. If you want to use the opportunity of your visit to ride in one of these and experience an *authentic* Alaskan experience similar to what is seen in movies, read on!

ALASKA BUSH PLANES

If you have ever watched a movie set in Alaska, you have likely seen bush planes being used. This is because bush planes are more than just a means of transportation; they are an  Alaskan way of moving around. The main reason for this is the limitation of the roads throughout the year, which means that the bush planes are ideal for reaching remote areas within the state. "Equipped with wheels, skis, or floats, bush aircraft are capable of landing on lakes, rivers, riparian gravel bars, beaches, and even in small clearings" (*Alaska Bush Aircraft*, n.d.).

Unlike commercial flights connecting airports worldwide, bush airplanes are used for shorter flights and require simpler infrastructure to operate. This makes them ideal for working in regions where transportation is limited for both passenger and cargo movement. They have a reinforced structure to deal with the more strenuous characteristics of the regions where they are used and an increased capacity compared to their size.

Nevertheless, some precautions need to be taken when riding one. You will need to limit your luggage and expect to have limited space, thus needing to be aware of the suitcases you are carrying. In many cases, if the luggage is too heavy, you might need to leave it behind, and it will reach you by traveling on a separate trip.

Finally, one last thing you must consider is that many of these planes are not as fancy or as new as the commercial planes many fly in. These airplanes are older and may suffer from weather interference, but this does not mean they are less safe. Nonetheless, you should be aware that these planes are more susceptible to turbulence, and you might experience some airsickness. Also, due to its open characteristics, remember to dress in warm layers, even on hotter days, since the temperature can be quite cold while flying.

LOCAL TRANSPORTATION

Those who fly into Alaska or do not rent a car will need to rely on the state's public transportation systems to get around. While this might not be too much of an inconvenience within the larger cities, the options might be quite limiting in smaller towns and more remote areas. In many cases, you will need to use a ride-share, private transportation, or take a bus to get where you want to go.

In many cases, public transportation can also be limited in frequency, so you must plan ahead if you are on a schedule. In addition to this, you will also have to consider the limitations of where this service travels and what happens during inclement weather conditions. However, if this is the method you'd like to use to get around, here is an overview of some of the main cities in the state and the public transportation available within them:

- **Anchorage:** It is served by the People Mover, a high-speed, 100% electric transit system connecting Anchorage's downtown and airport. The city has the state's most extensive public transportation system, and several thousand people use it to get around. In addition, there is also a bus service that covers various city parts and connects it to other cities. Another service the city offers is Ride-share, a carpool service for five people or more that helps those living in Anchorage commute to other areas on an agreed time and day. Lastly, the city has private transportation, such as taxis and app services, to help you move around. In this case, it is also important to watch for wait times since they can be in high demand in peak seasons.
- **Bethel:** This town has a smaller bus system with 30 lines serving the city, usually with a one-hour interval in between. Tickets are budget-friendly, ranging between $2–$3 for single-ride fares, $5 for day passes, and $30–$60 for monthly passes. Children up to 3 years old and those over 65 do not need to pay fares. Visitors can also use a shared-ride

taxi system, accessible by ferry through the Alaska Marine Highway system, apart from the bush planes service.

- **Fairbanks:** Although a smaller town, Fairbanks does have a local bus service, but it is worth mentioning that its routes are limited during the colder seasons. The Metropolitan Area Commuter System (MACS) is used and operates on eight routes, including to and from the airport. To get into and outside the city, you can travel to other cities by using the Alaska Railroad and the bus system.

- **Juneau:** The state's capital has a small, efficient, well-connected public transit system. It allows visitors to use the Alaska Marine Highway system and several buses to move around the city. Using these services makes it possible to move to and from the city and to move within; 10 routes serve residents and visitors. For several lines, the interval between buses can be up to one hour, so it will be essential to plan ahead and check the local schedule to know when you will need to arrive at the stops.

- **Ketchikan:** The public transportation system in the town, as in many others in Alaska, is connected by a bus route and the ferry system. Similarly to other cities, operation might be limited due to weather conditions, and some routes might be closed during the winter. While the bus lines operate within one hour, a shuttle service also serves the city and passes through all the bus stops.

- **Seward:** The town offers a free shuttle. The route takes approximately 30 minutes to get around the city and is also used by many as a tour bus. Buses connect the city to nearby regions, also served by the railroad, airplanes, and the ferry system.

On the official website of the State of Alaska, you will find links that will give you an insight into the public transportation services offered within different cities. This will be the ideal tool to help you plan how to move around and get to other regions if you plan to stay in more than one place. Lastly, as we arrive at the final section of the chapter, you will learn about the last forms of transportation that should be considered and are widely used by those living in Alaska: walking and biking.

CONSIDERATIONS FOR WALKING AND BIKING IN ALASKAN TOWNS

In many smaller towns, one of the main transportation methods for those living there is walking and cycling. There is a very active local biking scene and places where visitors can rent bikes and equipment to explore. Many of these stores will also offer guided tours for groups who want to ride bikes or hike. Surprisingly, many larger cities, such as Anchorage, only have a few walking possibilities within the city apart from the downtown areas. In this case, the major attraction will be the trails outside the towns, which will be the perfect experience to watch wildlife up close.

In fact, this is exactly what you will explore in the next chapter. As you read, you will discover some of the main species that live in the state and what makes it so attractive to them.

For example, did you know that Alaska offers one of the best opportunities for bear-watching? Several companies offer tours just for this! If you are excited about the possibility and want to learn how to (safely) get as close as possible to these animals, read on!

DO SOMETHING WILD TODAY!

> *The sweeping landscape of Alaska is like a painter's canvas waiting to be filled with vibrant colors of summer flowers and snow-capped mountains.*

— MEGAN EAVES

E njoying the wilderness is one of the main attractions for those visiting Alaska. Therefore, it is only natural that when visiting the state, one of the desired activities is to spot wildlife and see these animals in their natural habitats. If this is your objective, then you are in luck! This chapter will serve as a comprehensive guide, spotlighting prime locations for bear viewing in different regions, listing the top 10 wildlife encounters, and providing essential tips for safely observing Alaska's untamed inhabitants.

WHY IS ALASKA SO RICH IN WILDLIFE?

Being largely unexplored and having remote regions that are commonly inaccessible to humans are two of the main reasons why Alaska has such abundant wildlife. Additionally, the expansive protected areas and the lack of development in many of its regions allow wildlife to live in a sanctuary-like environment where they are free to roam and explore. This diversity and abundance are central to the Alaskan economy since many people visit the state for these experiences.

According to the Alaska Department of Fish and Game (2024), "Over 1,000 vertebrate species are found in the state, sometimes in huge numbers. More than 900,000 caribou roam in 32 herds across vast tundra landscapes." Some species that can be found within the state's boundaries include moose, bison, foxes, wolves, coyotes, deer, and, of course, bears, which are at the top of the food chain in the state. At the same time, marine animals also exist in abundance, including sea otters, sea lions, beavers, dolphins, whales, and walruses.

Preserving these species is a continuous effort by the population and the authorities, with a special mention to the National Park Service (NPS). Preserving the region's natural composition and diversity is one of its main activities, along with ensuring that "these areas offer unique opportunities to conduct scientific studies on natural systems and can serve as a sentinel for changes impacting our world" (*Wildlife in Alaska*, 2022).

If your main objective in visiting the state is to observe wildlife, following the specific guidelines is essential. In many cases, visitors unaware of best practices and what should be done can disturb the local habitat and put themselves, the group, and the animals in danger. Therefore, it is essential to observe some rules for safely observing wildlife and making the best of the experience.

TIPS FOR SAFELY OBSERVING WILDLIFE

If you are interested in observing wildlife in their natural habitats, here are a few tips you should consider to have the best experience while also keeping safe:

- **Keep your distance.** You should not get too close to wildlife—they might charge at you.
- **Stay away from young animals.** Although the smaller animals might be cute, and there is the temptation to touch them, you should not since their parents might be nearby.
- **Do not take your pets.** Observing wildlife requires discipline, and since pets might react negatively to the wildlife or even kill them, they must be restrained.
- **Wear appropriate clothing and footwear.** As you explore and look for wildlife, you will likely do a lot of walking and hiking. This means you want to wear warm clothes and sturdy hiking boots to ensure that you are protected.
- **Do not feed wildlife.** Visitors must not offer food or give the animals anything, including fishing for them,

to prevent wildlife from being influenced by the knowledge that if they approach humans, they will be fed. When observing wildlife, it is essential to interfere as little as possible with their activities.

- **Travel in groups.** Animals who see people arriving in groups are less likely to attack. Your group should ideally have more than three people.
- **Bring adequate equipment.** You should bring a telescopic lens for your camera or binoculars to have the best views since keeping a distance from the animals is essential. If you are going out in the wild, remember to bring bear spray with you in case you come close to one.
- **Leave no trace.** Remember the principle of leaving no trace if you go out in the wild. This means picking up after yourself and not removing anything.
- **Do not interfere with animal activity.** As you observe wildlife, they might be taking care of their offspring, eating, mating, or sleeping. Regardless of what they are doing, you should not try to get their attention.
- **Be observant and alert.** While visiting the outdoors for animal observation, it is essential to keep alert. Doing so will prevent both scaring the animals and being in danger. While making noise while you walk is important, you should not be so loud that you cannot hear what is happening around you.

As you can see, in many cases, the use of common sense when out in the wild looking at animals is the best course of action. At the same time, when your objective is to view them, it is essential to understand the best times to do so. For example, bears usually hibernate during the winter, so it is unlikely that you will spot them then. If you visit during the spring, you will likely see the animals with their cubs looking for food and teaching them how to hunt. Read on to discover the best opportunities for when to spot bears and have the experience of a lifetime!

A GUIDE TO BEAR VIEWING

Although it is possible to view bears in the wild, especially near water sources where they will be hunting for salmon, there are specialized companies that offer these experiences for those who want to have a greater possibility of these encounters occurring. If you want to join one of these tours, they usually depart from the larger cities, such as Anchorage, Kodiak, Homer, and Juneau. With these, you will be able to participate in expeditions for "visiting top bear viewing destinations like Brooks Falls at Katmai National Park, Kodiak National Wildlife Refuge, Lake Clark National Park,

Denali National Park, and Pack Creek Bear Viewing Area" (*Bear Viewing in Alaska*, 2024).

If you are set on seeing bears, you need to visit during the spring, summer, or fall when they are roaming the land and active in their habitats. During fall, bears look more actively for food as they prepare for hibernation. Because of this, they are more likely to be found near water looking for fish. Fall is also a good season to visit since there are fewer crowds. Finally, during the early spring, you may spot the first animals coming out of hibernation. However, this might be more challenging because they are focused on feeding and teaching the cubs. Nonetheless, despite these limitations, if you are traveling with a specialized bear-viewing company, they can take you to the spots where the chances are higher.

If bear viewing is a top priority for you during your trip to Alaska, you are about to discover the best ways to tick it off your list.

Bear-Viewing Guide and Companies

Alaska has the largest bear population in the United States, concentrating 98% of the brown bear population, 100,000 black bears, and between 4,000 and 7,000 polar bears (Stabinska, 2023). These bears are usually found near the water, on the coast, and there is also a significant number of them in the Kodiak Archipelago, where they are isolated from humans. Although visitors can see the animals independently by trying their luck in national parks or engaging in guided tours, you might need extra money in your budget if you want to embark on the latter.

This is because while independent bear viewing is mainly based on chance and how you explore the areas (on foot or by car), the opposite will likely occur when you have a guided tour. In this case, many companies do their best to offer the visitor a unique bear-viewing experience, which can include bush plane flights to reach the more remote regions. The price can be rather steep since the number of people is usually limited to six to seven people. In many cases, these tours can start at $200 per person for the simplest tour to over $1,000 for groups and an experience that includes food, beverages, and multiple stops.

Here are some of the places where you will be able to find these animals if you are planning on exploring independently:

- **Denali National Park:** This park is accessible by road and can be found halfway on the path between Anchorage and Fairbanks. If you want to observe grizzly bears, this is the best place since almost 400 bears live within its premises. Although navigating the park with your own car is restricted, you can hop on the bus tours operated by the park and spot them out in the wild.

- **Gates of the Arctic National Park:** Also home to many grizzly bears, this park will offer the possibility of observing polar bears when they prepare to hunt. Since this is a wilderness park, no roads lead to them or within the park, meaning you will need to arrive by plane. Most of the tours leave from Fairbanks and will stop in nearby communities where you will be able to access the park. Since the park is extensive and there are no roads, be sure to travel in groups or with a guided tour since if help is needed, it might take a while to arrive and find you.

- **Katmai National Park:** This park has the largest concentration of brown bears, with over 2,000 that can be seen as you explore the park. One of the main areas to observe the animals is near Brooks River Falls, where they are fishing or bathing. Since the park is not accessible by car, visitors must arrange transportation (plane or boat) from nearby locations. Due to the high number of visitors wanting to observe bears and the limited spots for camping on the grounds, most people will only have the opportunity for a day visit.

- **Kodiak Island:** With over 3,000 brown bears that have unique characteristics due to their adaptation to the island, Kodiak Island has almost 2 million acres to be explored to see the animals. In this case, the bears are rather big, some weighing more than 1,000 pounds and reaching almost 10 feet when standing. Reaching the island can only be done by plane or boat, and you can find a place to stay (if reserved ahead of time) in the small town of Kodiak.

- **Lake Clark National Park:** This remote park can only be reached by plane or boat. But once you are there, you will be able to see brown bears and other wildlife in their natural habitat. Since the park is rather big, it is recommended that people participate in guided tours to have a better chance of watching the animals.

If taking a guided bear tour sounds like something you want to explore, here are five companies worth considering during your research: Alaska Bear Adventures, Alaska Tours, Bear Viewing in Alaska, Kodiak Brown Bear Center, and Smokey Bay Air.

Although these are five very popular companies in the area, don't feel like you need to choose one from this list. Make sure you focus on finding the best one to serve your specific needs (budget, time, space) for the trip. Before booking or paying, read the contract and know the terms and conditions, including what you can and cannot do.

HUNTING AND FISHING OPPORTUNITIES IN ALASKA

Another great attraction for those visiting Alaska is participating in hunting and fishing expeditions organized by private individuals or companies. Since there is such an abundance of wildlife in the state, many want to visit to participate in the unique experience that fishing and hunting in Alaska offers. All this is possible in on-land establishments or marine tours while enjoying the amazing scenery and observing the protected wildlife.

In this final section of the chapter, you will explore all the possibilities for hunting and fishing in the state, including the different permits you might need for the activities you want to participate in, the best places to carry them out, and even what is allowed and what is not. In the last part, you will learn about some companies offering guided cruises, tours, and expeditions for these activities to help you streamline your search for the best company. Read on if you are ready to see what else Alaska has for you!

Fishing Overview

With over 6,500 miles of coastline, Alaska has plenty of opportunities for fishing. In addition, the great variety of fish in the region makes the activity even more fascinating. Today, many people visit the region looking to fish for one of the five types of salmon in its water: king, red, chum, pink, and silver salmon, along with halibut, which are also very common in the region. Traditionally, salmon season in the state begins in early to mid-June and goes until September, when the weather gets colder.

Whether you are interested in fly or traditional fishing, most areas will offer multiple options. This also includes different fishing locations since, in Alaska, it is possible to go saltwater, river, and deep sea fishing. Bristol Bay is one of the most well-known areas for fishing, with some of the world's biggest salmon and all species present. "June and July are best for king (Chinook) salmon, red sockeye salmon, and chum salmon. Later in the season, silver Coho salmon and pink humpback salmon are in plenty" (*Top 5 Fishing Destinations, 2017*).

For those interested in catching halibut, most major coastal cities have opportunities for this type of fishing. Some of the best places to go, in my experience are the Homer, Seward, Ninilchik, Soldotna, Kenai, Ketchikan, Valdez, and Juneau. In these places, you can find halibut that can easily reach up to 30 inches and weigh up to three digits (although experienced halibut fishermen will tell you that "chickens", or halibut between 20-30 pounds taste the best). If you do not know any locals, joining a guided tour will help you find the best spots for halibut fishing.

If you are visiting a national park and intend to go fishing, it is essential to check the park's regulations first to see if that is allowed.

Although there is high fish availability in Alaska, fishing is controlled when carried out by visitors, and you will need a license, especially for those looking to fish salmon. The license cost can be up to $100, but if you plan on catching King Salmon, you must pay an additional $45.00 for the king stamp. Each region has different regulations on the practice, and the prices can vary. Before going, check out the Alaska Department of Fish and Game webpage to see what regulations you need to follow.

Each region usually has a subregion where you will find all the information. In Prince William Sound, for example, in the southeast, fishing is limited to two king salmon per day and four in possession. Depending on the species you catch, there might be size restrictions. The regulations will usually describe what is allowed and what is not for fresh and salt-water. In addition, you will also find the locations where the practice can occur in these documents and all the necessary information, including the price for fishing licenses and how to obtain them.

Hunting Overview

The possibility of hunting large game such as moose and bear is another attraction that leads many people to select Alaska as their destination. However, several regulations must be followed to practice this sport in the state. The first is to obtain a hunting license, which allows you to go on expeditions. You must also buy the locking tags for the big game you are looking to hunt, which are placed on the animal as soon as it is killed and removed only after it is processed.

Each region will have a particular guideline for the seasons and the bag limits that are allowed to be taken. In this case, the state is divided into 26 regions, and the interested parties should consult the Alaska Department of Fish and Game to identify the rules for their region. Nonresidents of the state, regardless of age, are required to have a license and should provide a hunter's harvest ticket or permit when required.

Unlike fishing, nonresidents cannot go big-game hunting on their own. In these cases, each type of animal you desire to hunt will have a specific rule, such as the need to be accompanied by a licensed guide or resident and a contract to be signed. For those who are American citizens (referred to as *nonresidents*), different rules may apply to those who are not (referred to as *nonresident aliens*), and checking the rules for each situation is essential.

As soon as the animal is killed and locked, reporting the harvest using the appropriate form will be essential. This process can be done online or by mail, and not doing so will prevent you from obtaining a license in the future and will carry heavy fines. Since most of those interested in hunting big animals will need to hire a guide, it is only natural that you are probably wondering what the differences are between hiring a guide or putting a group together.

In the final part of this section, we will explore each of these, learning about their advantages and disadvantages, average prices, and opportunities for finding big game. You will also read some tips on the best ways to adventure on your own and recommendations for having a successful expedition.

Doing It on Your Own vs. Guided Options

The main differences between preparing for a hunting or fishing journey by yourself versus using a guided option are the cost and the efforts you will have to make. Although it is possible to obtain the licenses, gear, and locks on your own when you are looking to hunt or fish, if you do not want the trouble of having to find the appropriate material and run after the documentation, the best way to do it is to hire a specialized company. In this case, you will need to spend some time on the Alaska Department of Fish and Game webpage to be aware of all the procedures that must be carried out.

Another element you should keep in mind is that when you go on your own or with a guide with less knowledge, you might not find the appropriate area for the best hunting. In this case, the person guiding you will need to know where the game you intend to hunt is located and be familiar with the safety protocols to ensure that all goes well. At the same time, you will need to provide all the necessary additional items, such as transportation and food. To many just looking to have a good time, this can be a hassle that can be avoided by contacting a specialized company.

Hiring a guided tour comes with several benefits. Despite being a significantly more expensive option, ranging from $200 for a single-day trip to up to $7,000 for multiple days, there are more possibilities you will find the correct spot that will bring you results. In addition, they will also be aware of the laws and regulations you will need to follow. Some companies will even provide you with the necessary equipment and documentation to engage in the practice. If you are taking a multiple-day trip, they will also take care of finding any lodging and transportation needed for the trip, decreasing the efforts you would need to make if you were organizing it yourself.

If you plan to visit during the high season, you will likely have to reserve a spot with one of these companies well in advance of your trip since many people are interested in participating. Many companies will ask for a 50% deposit to save your spot and offer different add-ons that can be included in the price. As you look through the possibilities each of these companies offers, read the terms and conditions to ensure that all the necessary elements are included. Here are some companies worth checking out:

- Alaska Bush Flying Adventures
- Alaska Fishing Trips
- Arctic North Guides
- Green Rocks Lodge
- Hunting the World.com
- Kodiak Wilderness Adventures
- MacMillan River Adventures
- Mike Odin's Alaska Adventures
- River Rock Lodge
- Serenity Adventures

Finally, it is important to note that with all of these companies, there is no guarantee that you will be successful in your hunting or fishing expedition. They will do their best to provide you with the best conditions and possibilities to reach the best area. Still, they cannot guarantee that you will catch a fish or kill an animal. While many of these companies have the necessary expertise to guide and show you to the best places, it is important to remember that you are dealing with live animals with habits that can also change.

Now that you have explored some of the best possibilities for seeing wildlife in the state, it is time to look at another of the gems you will be able to experience: the Alaskan culture. With deeply rooted traditions seen in their festivals, decorations, and arts, you are about to discover the possibilities of immersing yourself in the local culture. As you will see, depending on the time you go or where you stay, you can enjoy some legitimate Alaskan experiences with the locals.

Join me in the next chapter as we discover what Alaska can offer visitors looking to immerse themselves in this unique environment. You will learn about the cultural heritage and the importance of celebrations to the Alaskan people and even see where you can ride on a dog sled, regardless of the time you visit. If you are ready to explore the richness and variety of the people and the place, read on! I am sure you will be enchanted by what you are about to learn.

EXPERIENCING ALASKA'S NATIVE CULTURE

> It's like the edge of the world here in Alaska; it has a
> rugged beauty that is incomparable.

— KAREN WALKER

Alaska has a unique combination of cultures and traditions. Whether learning about ancient Alaskan history and traditions by participating in one of its festivals or visiting one of its Native Heritage Centers, you will have ample opportunity to learn when you visit Alaska. As you navigate the state's traditional arts, lifestyles, culinary, and customs, you will see that these communities offer a truly unique experience.

In this chapter, you will learn about all the amazing opportunities to immerse yourself in the Alaska Native culture. You will learn about the best attractions and events to participate in depending on when you visit and how long you stay. Finally, you will learn all about the state's world-renowned traditional dogsled races. Let's explore what Alaska offers and all the cultural insight you will gain when visiting.

THE RICH HISTORY AND TRADITIONS OF ALASKA NATIVE COMMUNITIES

With a history of more than 10,000 Alaska Native communities, many of which are still in existence, there are many different options for visitors want to learn about the culture and its traditions. Generally speaking, Alaska Native people are divided into five groups that are separated by region: "Iñupiat & St. Lawrence Island Yup'ik in the Arctic; Athabascan in Southcentral and Interior Alaska; Yup'ik &

Cup'ik, Unangax̂ and Sugpiaq (Alutiiq) in Southwest Alaska; and Eyak, Haida, Tsimshian, and Tlingit in the Inside Passage" (*Alaska Native Culture*, n.d.).

One of the most significant characteristics of these people is their dedication, almost reverence, to the land and their traditions. This is important because many of the names of rivers and mountains you will see as you visit are influenced by these Native people, who represent a significant part of the state's population. About 15 percent of Alaska's 730,000 residents are Alaska Native, with 20 distinct cultures and 300 different dialects. Many Alaska Native people live in villages scattered along the coastline and rivers of Alaska (*Alaska Native Culture*, n.d.).

Traditional Arts and Crafts

Much of Alaska's culture is based on its vast and varied artistic expressions. In many communities, you will be able to learn more about these traditions through how these individuals express themselves: dance, singing, basketry, beadwork, carving, music, and weaving. In many instances, visitors can participate in these activities and learn more about how the traditions are passed from person to person.

One of the most significant traditions that Alaska Natives carry out is the practice of storytelling and sharing myths and legends across generations. It is the elders' job to tell these stories and educate the younger people on the traditions and the culture of the people of the past and how they influence the present. Usually, this storytelling activity involves music and dancing, often done in elaborate regalia and masks that help to tell a story (*Arts & Traditions*, n.d.).

By using these traditions and customs, residents and visitors alike can learn more about the people who have inhabited the state for thousands of years. This is a way to keep their traditions alive and show how important their heritage is to them, which you will also notice as you travel.

While they also create artwork that is available for sale, most Alaska Native people live subsistence lifestyles that respect the land where they live and the animals with which they share the space.

Subsistence Lifestyles

For Alaska Native communities, respecting the land means using it responsibly and protecting it from degradation. In many cases, members of this community will hunt, fish, and forage to maintain their homes and create traditional recipes unique to their culture. These subsistence practices not only strengthen ties between people and nature—they are especially critical for Alaska Native families in remote and rural areas as a means of providing food security, economic stability, and nutrition (Travel Alaska, 2024).

Although many traditions are kept, they are associated with and supplemented by modern technology to help them increase their production while maintaining their traditions. As a part of their diets, they consume elements they gather on the land, such as berries, eggs, mushrooms, salmon, moose, deer, caribou, king crab, and even birds. Alaska Natives are the only people in the U.S. that are also allowed to hunt whales and polar bears for subsistence. Harvesting all of these animals and plants is usually done responsibly, with the least possible environmental interference, and producing the least waste possible.

Waste of any amount is considered disrespectful to Alaska Natives. These people use all the elements they can extract from the animals. They will use the feathers and hides to create clothes and accessories, even using them in their crafts. In most cases, everything the animal provides when killed for feeding purposes will be used or eaten since they believe waste is disrespectful to both the animal and the people who depend on it (Travel Alaska, 2024).

Traditional Ecological Knowledge

With thousands of years of experience, Alaska Natives have extensive knowledge about the land, animals, and plants of the region. This traditional ecological knowledge results from information being passed down through generations, which often helps researchers and scientists with their studies. The ancestral knowledge gathered throughout the years helps these communities have a deeper understanding of the region's history, science, and what the land can offer.

Much of this traditional knowledge helps other generations learn how to develop nutritious dishes and clothes to keep individuals warm through the rigorous winter. This can also be seen in the local architecture, in understanding climate forecasts and changes, the best seasons for harvesting and planting, and in identifying archaeological sites to understand how previous people lived (National Park Service, 2021). In many places, it is possible to obtain important historical data associated with traditions that have been gathered through time, creating a more diverse and rich cultural experience for visitors to learn and enjoy.

ALASKA NATIVE ATTRACTIONS AND CULTURAL EXPERIENCES

For those interested in learning more about Alaska Native culture and history, there are several opportunities to do so at one of many attractions. One reason for this is that local culture is extensively celebrated through museums, cultural tours, demonstrations, and activities you can partake in. Alaska has over 60 museums and cultural centers statewide dedicated to showing local culture and enabling people to understand the importance of these people to the state's history.

In this section, you will have an overview of the most popular heritage center dedicated to Alaska Native culture and some tours you can enjoy according to each region you will be in. You will learn about the experiences you can participate in and how to increase your knowledge of these secular traditions that are still practiced. Finally, you will learn about one of the most unique traditions in the state, dog mushing.

To learn about all the opportunities you can enjoy during your visit, you can lookup local news sites online before you visit or get a copy of the local newspaper as soon as you arrive. Many cultural events, visitation, and immersive opportunities will be listed. In many cases, there will be seasonal activities, which means you will likely have a once-in-a-lifetime opportunity to experience the full extension of Alaska Native tradition.

Alaska Native Heritage Center

Located in Anchorage, the Alaska Native Heritage Center is one of the most well known places in the state dedicated to the history of its Native people. In it, you can explore traditional arts and stories, meet carvers, and watch performances. It is a center where history is not just here to be observed; visitors can live it and engage in traditional activities such as speaking to artists and elders, learning one of the Native languages, or even participating in crafts classes.

Although most things to do are inside the heritage center, those who see it from the outside immediately feel the power of the Alaska Native culture. One of the buildings surrounding it is a traditional Southeast Alaska Log House that usually accommodates several families. Inside, it is possible to see life-sized traditional posts carved by artisans from four different communities. Each post is carved and painted with a different theme of respect: respect for family, environment, culture, and self (*Alaska Native Heritage Center*, n.d.).

Visitors interested in exploring more of the Alaska Native culture can find the heritage center at 8800 Heritage Center Dr., which is open throughout the summer from 9 a.m. to 5 p.m. and is closed during the winter until mid-April. Visitors pay between $19 and $30; private tours cost $150 and have a capacity of 20 people.

Cultural Tours and Demonstrations

Since many tourists who visit Alaska are interested in learning more about its rich and traditional culture, several Alaska Native-led tours and demonstrations are offered. In many cases, visitors will be taken to watch a traditional dance or music performance, participate in artistic and creative activities, and explore the local architecture. Specialized offers for these activities exist in almost all state regions, including Ketchikan, Sitka, Kodiak Island, and Glacier Bay.

Visitors are encouraged to hire local companies that offer services to support the communities to which they belong. By doing so, you will also have a higher possibility of learning about the culture and the traditions as you explore and hear stories directly from the mouths of those who have heard these stories from their elders.

Finally, if you are lucky, you will be able to book a tour which also includes a visit to local buildings where you can go inside and look around and have the opportunity to taste the unique Alaska Native cuisine. In most cases, the people receiving tourists are more than happy to talk about their culture and share their traditions. You might even learn a few words in one of the dialects and come back with something new to show!

Dog Mushing Traditions

Another Native Alaska tradition that you should look out for is dog mushing. Traditionally carried out in the region of Fairbanks, where the Athabascan and Iñupiaq people introduced the practice, you will have the opportunity to learn more about the practice and its different styles. Dog mushing is culturally significant for these communities, especially during late winter and early spring.

Speaking about traditions and events, if you plan to be in the region around mid-March, you will have the unique opportunity to watch dog mushing teams from around the world gather for the Dog Mushing Open North American Championship. The competition is known as "the longest continuously run sled dog race in the world" (Alaska Dog Mushers Association, 2024). On the event page, you can watch the competition and register to participate in the race if all criteria are met.

Many Alaska Native traditional festivals are held around the state throughout the year. From February to November, you can participate in fairs and cultural and sports events and watch presentations on local traditions. If you want to ensure that you participate in one while visiting or plan your trip around a specific event, read on to learn more about when these are held and what to expect.

ALASKA TRADITIONAL EVENTS

Regardless of the season in which you are visiting, there will always be different things for you to do. From sports events to cultural activities, there are over 20 different experiences to choose from below. As you might imagine, June and July have the most activities. However, February and April are not far behind. Here is a quick list with some of the monthly events you can attend (there are many others, usually announced by local news outlets) so that you can guarantee tickets before arriving.

January

- Alcan 200 Snowmachine Race (Haines)
- Anchorage Folk Festival (Anchorage)

February

- Alaska Folk Festival (Juneau)
- Festival of Native Arts (Fairbanks)
- Fur Rendezvous (Anchorage)
- Kivgiq—Messenger Feast (Anchorage)
- Séet Ká Festival (Petersburg)
- World Ice Championship (Fairbanks)

March

- Fur Rondy Charlotte Jensen Artist Market (Anchorage)
- **Iditarod Sled Dog Race & Art Show (Anchorage)**
- World Eskimo-Indian Olympics (WEIO) (winter)
- World Ice Championship (Fairbanks)

April

- Native Youth Olympics (NYO) (Anchorage)
- Northern Regional Traditional Games (Juneau)
- Slush Cup (Alyeska)
- Spring Carnival (Girdwood)
- Stikine River Birding Festival (Wrangell)

May

- Kodiak Crab Fest (Kodiak)
- May Day Fly-In Air Show (Valdez)

June

- Mayor's Marathon (Anchorage)

- Midnight Sun Run (Fairbanks)
- Nalukataq—Spring Whaling Celebration (Utqiaġvik)
- PrideFest (Anchorage)
- Qatnut Arctic Trade Fair (Kotzebue)
- Summer Solstice Festival (Anchorage)

July

- Bear Paw Festival (Anchorage)
- Copper River Salmon Jam (Cordova)
- Fairbanks Summer Arts Festival (Fairbanks)
- Forest Fair (Girdwood)
- Golden Days (Fairbanks)
- Midnight Sun Intertribal Powwow (Fairbanks)
- Mount Marathon (Seward)
- World Eskimo-Indian Olympics (WEIO) (summer)

August

- Alaska State Fair (Palmer)
- Anchorage RunFest (Anchorage)
- Tanana Valley State Fair (Fairbanks)

September

- Alaska State Fair (Palmer)
- Alaska World Arts Festival (Homer)
- Rubber Duck Race (Nome)

October

- Alaska Day Festival (Sitka)
- Indigenous Peoples Day (statewide)
- Shellfish Festival (Ketchikan)

November

- Alaska Bald Eagle Festival (Haines)
- Sitka WhaleFest (Sitka)

December

- Anchorage International Film Festival (Anchorage)
- Winter Arts Faire (Ketchikan)

As you read the list above, you likely noticed that the Iditarod Trail Sled Dog Race was marked in bold. No, this is not an editing mistake—it was on purpose because this is the one event we will explore further in the next section of this chapter. Being one of Alaska's most well-known and traditional events, it is held during March and is known as the "last great race on Earth." If you want to learn more about this amazing event and what makes it so popular, read on! If you haven't decided on when you are visiting, this may be the motivation you need to book your tickets!

IDITAROD TRAIL SLED DOG RACE

The history of this traditional race dates back to 1967 when it was still a short race of approximately 25 miles celebrating the centennial purchase of Alaska by the United States. Six years later, in 1973, it became the race it is known for today at almost 1,100 miles long, connecting the cities of Anchorage and Nome. The competition is so popular that it attracts over 100 participants of both sexes annually with their dog teams to see who could navigate the old Iditarod Trail dog sled mail route the fastest (Butcher, 2024).

According to Butcher (2024), the race was created in honor of a musher who participated in one of the state's most important historical events:

The trail declined in use in the 1920s, when the airplane began to replace the dogsled as the primary means of crossing the difficult terrain. But when no capable pilot was available during Alaska's diphtheria epidemic of 1925, a team of mushers battled blizzard conditions and rushed serum to icebound Nome. This heroic action called the "Great Race of Mercy," brought renewed international fame to the trail and the dog teams, particularly to Balto, the lead dog of the team that finally reached Nome.(para. 2)

One of the characteristics of this race is that despite starting in Anchorage, this is only a ceremonial start since the official beginning of the race is actually 70 miles north, in Willow. Those interested in the Iditarod Trail Sled Dog Race can place bids on the race's site between December and January for the opportunity to ride on the sled with the mushers as they are on their way to the official start place. Those with the highest bid will be able to secure a spot during the first miles of the event for an unforgettable experience.

If you are not among the lucky winners, don't worry! Other ways to participate in the race include following along with it on a snowmobile or on a plane or working as a volunteer.

If you choose to volunteer, you can help tend to the dogs, the participants, and the organization during its course. For those who want more "social" participation, it is possible to participate in the banquet offered to mushers before the race, which is a gala where mushers will draw their starting order and mingle with others.

Those interested in purchasing tickets or learning more about participating in one of the state's most iconic events can access the iditarod.com website, where you can even buy official merchandise from the online store. Additionally, when the race starts, you can follow along and see the results and updates on the page in real-time.

As you prepare to enter the last chapter of this first part, we will be discussing a subject that is essential to know when visiting Alaska: staying safe. Since many visitors want an outdoor experience and contact with nature, but do not have prior experience in these situations, there are certain precautions that should be taken to minimize safety issues as you travel. If you are ready to read about the must-dos and the don'ts, read on. While some certainly go without saying, others may surprise you.

STAYING SAFE IN THE MOUNTAINS

> *Nobody is accidentally in Alaska. The people who are in Alaska are there because they choose to be, so they've sort of got a real frontier ethic. The people are incredibly friendly, interesting, smart people—but they also stay out of each other's business.*

— MARCUS SAKEY

I t is not for nothing that Alaska is commonly referred to as "the last frontier." With much of its territory still unexplored and many beautiful remote areas to visit, it is essential that when visiting, tourists take precautions to ensure they stay safe. Sometimes, this might mean needing to pack extra gear, keeping your eyes open for wildlife while driving, and having alternative plans for visiting areas with fewer towns and people.

Because so much of this beautiful state is unsettled and remote, those planning on venturing on their own or in smaller groups need to pay attention to specific things that might make the difference between solving a problem and having a problem. In this chapter, you will learn how to stay safe in Alaska with a comprehensive guide full of outdoor tips and bear and general safety information essential for those visiting. As you navigate this chapter, take note of what's necessary in order for you to embrace Alaska's unique experiences while ensuring a safe and memorable adventure.

STAYING SAFE IN THE LAST FRONTIER

The first thing visitors must understand when visiting Alaska is that the state is unlike most traditional vacation destinations, not only because of its incredible traditions and culture and access to the outdoors but also because of its unique setup when it comes to transportation, technology, and accessibility. In the urban areas, you will likely not feel that much of a difference: Many of the larger and smaller towns are similar to what we are used to. However, when you venture out of these areas, keeping an eye open for everything around you is essential.

Preparedness and Planning

The first thing you should consider when planning to explore Alaska is preparing and planning in advance. This means that you should study the route you plan to take, obtain maps and extra batteries, have all the gear you need, and identify where you can stop, restock, or fill the gas tank. Since many of the state's remote areas have little to no internet and cell phone coverage, it is crucial to have a few paper maps that you have looked over and are familiar with and identify places where you can obtain help if necessary.

When packing, bring the appropriate clothing and shoes, survival kits for emergencies, and the necessary navigation tools that do not need to be constantly charged. Ideally, before traveling, let at least one (preferably more) person know where you are going, the route you plan to take, the expected time you will reach your destination, and when you are expected to return. If where you are going has no internet and cell phone coverage, leave details of when you plan to come back and any of the places you are planning on stopping to visit. Finally, you should not travel on your own to remote areas. If something happens, it can take help a long time to reach you, if it can reach you at all.

Weather Conditions

Although you should always do your best to prepare, this does not mean you can predict everything, and the weather is one of these things. Despite being a place where it is easy to identify the year's seasons, this does not mean the weather is not extreme or doesn't suddenly change. While it is never scorching hot during the summer, and in fact, the temperatures can be rather mild, ranging between 55–70 $^\circ$F throughout the day, the weather can significantly drop during the night because of the winds that come from the water. So, even if you are traveling from June to August, you should be sure to pack some warm clothes just in case the weather suddenly becomes colder.

The same can be said about inclement weather. If you are exploring on your own or even driving, it is essential to check the weather reports before you leave to ensure that there will be no unforeseen circumstances. If the weather is terrible, but leaving is necessary, you should take the time to identify potential stopping points, gas stations, and nearby towns on the route you are taking in case of any emergencies. It is important, especially when the weather is bad, to listen to the local radio stations to learn about the current road conditions and anything you might face on your trip.

Pay attention to incoming fog, if the winds are too strong, and if visibility might be affected. Especially when driving, low visibility and weather disturbances can cause accidents due to avalanches, roadblocks, sliding on the road, and even encountering and hitting wildlife roaming in the area. When there are challenging weather conditions, the probability of an accident increases significantly due to the possibility of natural hazards and the driver's lack of experience driving under the same circumstances.

Dress for the Weather

Knowing how to protect yourself in cold weather is important and can be life-saving. The cold weather that can be experienced in the Alaskan wilderness, regardless of the season, can be fatal if you are not properly dressed to keep warm. When this happens, you might suffer from hypothermia, which is the body's lack of ability to keep warm. If this happens, you will not be able to help yourself because hypothermia impedes your ability to reason and eventually will cause you to lose consciousness, making it crucial to have someone with you to help.

To prevent this from happening, it is essential that you keep your clothes dry and that you are dressed in layers. This means wearing the appropriate clothing for the activity engaged in. You should always have a coat with you in case of need and a change of clothes (and socks) in case yours get wet. If possible, your clothes should be water- and wind-resistant. In all circumstances, it is better to be able to peel off the layers in case you get warm than not having enough clothes to prevent being cold.

If you are traveling long distances, remember to keep blankets inside the car if you need to spend the night inside. If there is another person or people with you, getting physically near each other and huddling up is recommended so that your bodies stay warm. If you do not have the appropriate gear to camp or start a fire, you should stay in the vehicle. Eat periodically and try to have a thermos with some warm food or liquids and plenty of water to stay hydrated.

Avoiding Natural Hazards

Whether you are staying near the coast or going into more remote areas, it is essential to be cautious and aware of the natural hazards you might face. If you are traveling through the coast, it is essential to check for muddy areas, potential floods, and rising tides. Areas knows as "mud flats" in several areas of the state are extremely dangerous to traverse. Mud flats are muddy areas that are exposed when the tide is out. I lived in Alaska for 16 years, and I can personally recall at least a dozen reports of people walking onto the flats, getting stuck in the mud, and drowning when the tide came in. So, do not enter! At the same time, these coastal areas might have rocks and other unstable grounds that might prove to be a safety hazard, especially if the smaller rocks start rolling. In this case, it might mean that there is unstable ground near you.

Awareness of potential landslides and avalanches is essential to staying safe when visiting remote areas. At the same time, not getting too close to rugged landscapes and staying away from areas with too much snow can also save you a lot of trouble. When traveling through these areas, the ideal approach, if you do not know the terrain, is to hire a knowledgeable guide to help you through the area.

Outdoor hazards are common in Alaska, especially in areas that few people travel through and there may be very little maintenance. Therefore, the more you avoid these potentially dangerous areas, the safer you will be. If you are driving with another person or even a group and not taking a guide, it is recommended that you obtain the most information possible about the route you will be taking and all the elements that should be considered to stay safe. Preparation is key to ensure your trip's success.

Campsite Safety

When you reach your destination safely and are planning on camping, there are some things that you should keep in mind to ensure you have the best experience. One of the first things you want to do before you leave is check that your tent is adequate, has no holes, and is waterproof. If it is, you also want to check that it has adequate ventilation and that you have enough space to place all your belongings and food when camping. Properly storing your items (especially food) will help guarantee that bears and other wildlife are not attracted to your site, which will help keep you safe. Make sure campfires are out before you go to sleep. Leave no trace of food in the area and that all your trash is disposed of. Try to leave as little of a trace as possible so that you do not interfere with wildlife's natural habitats or attract them to your campsite.

Usually, camping areas along the roads or in the parks have signage and a place to park. In some of these camps, you might have the opportunity to stock up on supplies, appropriately discard your trash, and even dry your clothes. Some camps will allow you to stay without a fee, while others might charge a small amount.

Hiking Safety

One of the major attractions of exploring the outdoors in Alaska is the availability of hiking trails that are suitable for all ages and fitness levels. To ensure you have the best experience while doing so, study the trail you plan to take and stay on the designated path. You should remember to bring maps and navigation equipment as, once again, internet and cell phone coverage might be spotty or even nonexistent.

When packing for a hike, you should think about the estimated time it will take to complete the trail and the necessary gear you will need. This includes a jacket, adequate shoes, walking sticks, plenty of water, snacks, a map, and navigating tools. Whether you are going out alone (which is not recommended) or in a group, you should inform someone where you are going and the trail you plan to take. Ideally, you want a group of at least 3–4 people to go on the hike with you; if there is any trouble or an accident with someone in the group, one person can stay and care for them, and the others can look for help.

Remember that there are risks when hiking outdoors, especially when there are no defined trails, because you will not know what to expect. In this case, you should prioritize safety over reaching your intended destination, even if this means stopping halfway through and returning to where you started. Remember to check the weather and bring extra layers in case the climate changes and you need to keep warm.

Bring a First Aid Kit and Essentials

Considering that help may take some time to arrive in remote areas, you should bring a first aid kit to tend to minor emergencies. Bringing antiseptic, gauze, bandages, and other essential items can be crucial to helping stabilize yourself or another injured person. While many consider these unnecessary and "extra baggage," they can make a difference in an emergency.

In this case, we are talking about extra fuel, matches, or a lighter if you need to start a fire, a pocket knife, and other wilderness survival material. These items should also include an extra water bottle to fill up when you find a potable water source and food like protein and carb snacks that will help you keep your energy. By preparing in advance for the worst, it is possible to increase the chances of a successful outcome in adverse situations.

Lastly, while not life threatening, mosquitos and flies and be quite overwhelming in Alaska in the summer. Plan accordingly!

Survival Basics and Common Sense

Lastly, and this is important to remember, you should never doubt your ability to survive if something happens. Using common sense and knowledge of basic survival might be the difference in determining a successful outcome. Although most of us live in urban areas and are not as used to extreme circumstances, we must remember that we are humans and have an innate survival instinct within us. Mental toughness goes a long way. Using this and listening to your intuition will be crucial when you are out in the wild.

If you plan on camping and hiking for more than a couple of days in the wilderness, it is worth taking the time to learn about basic survival skills and inform yourself about the different strategies you can take. This means identifying potential edible and inedible plants, determining how to obtain water, and identifying other critical elements that will make a difference. Today, it is possible to find this information online, including downloadable manuals to take with you if needed.

Remembering to take all the necessary precautions before you leave, such as telling others where you will be, might be the difference between having a successful outing and not. At the same time, we must also consider that these survival techniques will depend on your encounters with wildlife. To help you prepare for these, the next section of this chapter will provide tips and precautions when out in the wild and what you should be aware of when exploring these areas.

BEAR AND OTHER WILDLIFE SAFETY TIPS AND PRECAUTIONS

Although having an experience with wildlife might be the high point of your trip to Alaska, remembering that these animals are not used to humans and might react aggressively is essential to guaranteeing that you or other members of your family are not harmed. I realize this sounds very obvious - but dozens of tourists are injured every year because they do not give wildlife a respectful berth and keep their distance. Although you have already been given some tips on dealing with these encounters in Chapter 3, here we will explore a few other things that must be considered if this occurs and what you should do to remain safe.

- **Carry bear spray.** This powerful product might be the difference between life and death while hiking in bear country. The product is made of capsaicin, which is what makes hot peppers hot. Remember that while carrying this product, it should be easily reachable and not somewhere you will have to look for it in case you need it. This means keeping it within reach, such as in your pocket or attached to your belt. When you buy it, you can obtain information at the store on how to use it and the best ways to use it if you encounter a bear.

- **Make noise.** Although you do not want to make loud noises that will disrupt wildlife when hiking, you should ensure that you are being loud enough that animals will be alerted to your presence. To make this noise, you can sing, clap your hands, talk loudly, or do anything else that will make your presence notable. Some people wearing some kind of bell or other "jingly" item on their person to accomplish this. When animals hear this, they expect something to happen, reducing the chances of a surprise encounter. Surprising a wild animal, especially a mother with young, is the worst mistake you can make in the wild.

- **Stay alert:** Knowing your surroundings is essential to preparing for a potential wildlife encounter. This means watching for animal tracks, listening to sounds, and observing signs of plant disturbance.

- **Avoid surprising bears and other animals.** If you see a bear or other animals, avoid surprising them. If it notices your presence and if it starts to get close, you should speak calmly and firmly so it knows you are human and not prey. In the case of bears, they should not be approached, and you should slowly back away while keeping an eye on them. If the animal is charging you, make sure your bear spray is ready to be used in case it gets too close. Most popular trail heads in Alaska have bear notices posted, so be on the lookout for those as well.

- **Store food properly.** If you are planning on longer hikes and even camping, it is essential that you properly store food and garbage in bear- or animal-resistant containers. If you stay overnight and do not have these containers, you should hang the supplies in a tree so they are at least 10 feet off the ground and 4 feet away from the trunk. This will help prevent bears and other animals from being attracted to your campsite.

- **Know how to react.** If an animal charges you, stand your ground and use your bear spray. If there is contact between the animal and you, you should fight back with anything at hand, such as rocks, sticks, or bear spray. Do not run, as this can trigger a chase response. In this case, not being alone will be crucial to your survival, as the other group members will be able to help fight the animal.

- **Other animals are dangerous too.** Bear safety is certainly important since a bear attack is usually deadly, but remember that pretty much any wild animal can be dangerous if it feels threatened. For example, moose charge and injure people every year in Alaska. So apply these tips to all wildlife encounters!

You now have all the necessary information to start your adventure. As we move on to the second part of this book, it is time to learn about Alaska's different regions and what you can explore in each one. As you navigate the other chapters, you will learn about the major local attractions, places to sleep and eat, and their unmissable opportunities. So get ready to start planning your trip!

PART II
REGIONS OF ALASKA

IF YOU ARE ENJOYING THIS BOOK, please consider leaving a review. Reviews from leaders like you help others identify resources for information, and when you leave a review you are supporting independent writers.

SOUTHCENTRAL ALASKA

> *Alaska isn't about who you were when you headed this way. It's about who you become.*

— KRISTIN HANNAH

Welcome to the most populated region in Alaska and home to its largest city, Anchorage. Here, you will find different opportunities to explore and enjoy the urban and the wild. Between the opportunities to enjoy the summer and the spring amidst colorful flowers or hike, ski, or sled during the winter, the region is the best place to start your Alaskan adventure. In this area, you will see the best of what Alaska offers: fishing, wildlife, shopping, culture, arts, entertainment, and lively nightlife.

If you are coming by plane, your flight may land here since Anchorage has the largest international airport in the state, with connecting flights, boats, and trains to other regions. As you prepare to explore, you will also learn the best places to stay, where to eat, and the best activities to make this trip memorable.

ANCHORAGE: ALASKA'S URBAN JEWEL

Anchorage is the most urban city in Alaska, where modernity gets mixed with tradition, and the concrete rises in the middle of the wilderness. Located between the Chugach Mountains and Cook Inlet, wilderness is just a short trip from downtown. In fact, as you cruise by the water, you can see the modern world on one side and its natural state on the other. Today, with almost 300,000 residents, it is possible to mix the desire for adventure with the need for comfort all in one trip.

Despite being a modern urban area, Anchorage's traditions, history, and culture are deeply rooted among the population. The Alaska Native Heritage Center, the Anchorage Museum, and the Alaska Aviation Heritage Museum are located here. Some of the major festivals in the state are held in this city, which means there will likely be opportunities for you to participate in one of them if you are staying in the area. Finally, surrounded by an incredible botanical garden and the fourth largest state park in the United States, Chugach State Park, you will feel that you have found a place where it is possible to have it all.

Those interested in shopping and getting to know its urban setting will find major retail stores mixed with local artisan shops that sell incredible crafts and products. This is also the perfect opportunity to taste some of the delicious local food in restaurants of all types, from simple diners to fancier settings. Salmon and halibut, both local delicacies, is offered in most places, along with other types of seafood as well as the exotic reindeer sausage.

Sports and adventure lovers will also enjoy the opportunity to explore while riding 4x4s in the wilderness, hiking trails, cycling across the city, taking boats for fishing and short cruises, and even kayaking, canoeing, and paddling as they visit. The city's temperature is mild compared to other regions since winter varies between 5–20 ºF, and in the summer, it is possible to enjoy warmer 60-70 ºF days, which are ideal for a T-shirt and a pair of shorts. Still, regarding the seasons, as you visit, it is important to remember that during the summer, the days are extended, with over 20 hours of sunlight, and that in the winter, this can be as short as five hours a day.

One of the most significant advantages of Anchorage is its easy connection to other regions. This means that visitors can catch a plane to sightsee or connect to more remote areas, take a boat to enjoy a cruise, or even rent a car to drive to nearby areas. The main railroad of the state also passes by the city, connecting it to other regions and allowing easy access even when the weather is bad. From the city, you will be able to explore many other areas in the Southcentral region, which we will discuss as we go through the chapter.

KENAI PENINSULA: OUTDOOR PARADISE

Located just a short trip south of Anchorage, the Kenai Peninsula has some of Alaska's main adventures in an area the size of West Virginia. There, visitors can find a national park, a traditional fishing village, wildlife on land and sea, see and learn about glaciers, and engage in almost all the outdoor activities you can think of. One of the best ways to explore the peninsula is to rent a car or an RV and go on a road trip, which will enable you to see the area's highlights and check off your bucket list most of the things you want to do in Alaska.

The first attraction you should consider visiting is the Kenai Fjords National Park, where incredible wildlife species can be explored. These include sea lions, orcas, and whales in the sea, bears, beavers, coyotes, and moose on land, and over 190 species of birds in the air. Due to its ranger and contractor-led activities, it will be possible to explore the park and its main attractions while learning about preservation and engaging in outdoor activities. Kayaking and hiking are common activities in the park, as well as sightseeing and closely exploring glaciers.

For more urban areas, the cities of Seward and Homer have a close connection to the state's history. While the first connects to the old railroad and is an important port town for those arriving by cruise, Homer is known for its fishing traditions and the incredible number of salmon and halibut available for the sport. Seward is a larger town than Homer, meaning there are more lodging opportunities and restaurants to enjoy. The Alaska SeaLife Center is located in Seward, which is one of Alaska most popular aquariums. On the other hand, the smaller Homer will offer a more relaxing environment and even the possibility of seeing bears due to its proximity to Kenai Fjords National Park.

If you plan on staying on the peninsula to explore, it is possible to see a lot in three to four days by spending a night in Seward and Homer and an additional one in Kenai Fjords to have the full experience. If you have an extra day, you might want to stop in Soldotna or Kenai, which are also smaller towns but will be right next to Kenai National Wild Refuge, where there are also bears to see. Taking this route makes it possible to see the best of what the state has to offer. As you drive between the regions, you will see that the estimate your GPS gives you for the route is almost impossible to make happen because of the amazing scenery and photo opportunities you will have on the way. If you are visiting during the summer, you will also need to be patient since it is a popular local destination and you might find some crowded roads along the way.

Author's tip: As you travel from Seward to Homer, take the opportunity to see the different glaciers that will appear throughout your trip. One of the most unique opportunities you will have is to visit Exit Glacier. This magnificent structure allows visitors to explore it on foot. For those interested in learning more about the glacier, there is an eight-hour guided tour leaving from Seward that will give you a glimpse of its waterfalls, holes, cracks, and other features.

MATANUSKA-SUSITNA VALLEY: ADVENTURES IN THE VALLEY

Located 45 minutes north of Anchorage, between the Chugach and Talkeetna mountains and the Alaska Range, lies the Matanuska-Susitna (Mat-Su) Valley. From there, visitors will have the first real view of Denali Mountain, the highest peak in the United States. With the several outdoor adventures in the region, it is possible to visit six state parks, including Denali State Park, which should not be confused with Denali National Park. Among the most popular cities in the region are Palmer, Willow, and Talkeetna, which attract the most tourists for lodging and eating.

The small town of Talkeetna is a tourist favorite because of its quaint appearance and easy access to Denali National Park, located just at its border. It is usually from there that visitors start their journey into the park by car or by plane. It is simply one of those places that, when visited, tourists fall in love with because of the friendly people and lovely environment. Especially popular during late spring and throughout the summer, those who plan on staying there should make reservations in advance. The only inconvenience is that due to its limited number of restaurants and diners, there will probably be a long wait time to eat no matter where you go. This can easily be solved by ordering your food to go and eating it by the river.

For those seeking an outdoor adventure, Talkeetna and other towns such as Palmer and Glacier View offer the opportunity to engage in zip lines that travel across the lakes, glaciers, and forests, as well as other outdoor experiences. One of these zip lines travels over 1,000 feet at almost 250 feet up. It is indeed a different experience to have. Those not meeting the requirements or looking for something else to do can enjoy horseback riding, rappelling, hiking, and biking tours.

Author tip: The Mat-Su Valley is a local favorite, so check availability when staying there. During the summer, many of Alaska's residents visit the region to enjoy their vacations in its rivers and mountains. If you want an outdoor experience with the locals to see how they enjoy their free time, this is certainly the place to be.

DENALI NATIONAL PARK: THE CROWN JEWEL OF THE INTERIOR

Reaching this national park, one of the state's main attractions, can be done by car, plane, boat, or train. The Denali National Park is located between Anchorage and Fairbanks at mile 237 of Highway 3. If you are arriving by train, there is a stop near the park's entrance, which may be a good alternative to sitting in the long traffic lines that are present during the warmer seasons. In fact, if you are okay with not driving into the park, using the local transportation available and the park's free shuttle to get here is your best bet, and you will avoid waiting.

Being in the park will allow you to see Mount Denali up close, learn about the region, and explore wildlife. Although its most popular season for visitors is summer, those who wish to engage in winter activities will find plenty to do in the park since it does not close for the season. The possibility of indoor picnicking, biking, snowshoeing, and skiing attracts some of those who want to stay away from the larger crowds and have a more private experience.

Denali National Park has three campgrounds and some externally run accommodations within its limits. Most of these are open throughout the year. If you plan on visiting, ensure you have all the information you need since there is limited to no cell phone coverage in the area, with Wi-Fi in limited restaurants and lodges. Whether you are camping or not, you will be able to enjoy the restaurants that are open inside and nearby, although most of them close during the lower season.

Author's tip: Before exploring the park, tourists who are unfamiliar with it should visit the Denali Visitor Center, located near the entrance. There, it will be possible to obtain a park map and talk to friendly rangers who will answer questions and give some of the park's highlights. You can also find information on tours and programs offered throughout the year, which is a great possibility if you want to explore in a guided manner. Also note that cars are not allowed very far into the park; you can only drive in 15 miles, in fact. From here, you must board a bus tour to venture further into the park.

PRINCE WILLIAM SOUND: A MARITIME WONDERLAND

To the southeast of Anchorage and bathing the Kenai Peninsula, you will find what can only be described as a maritime paradise. Here you will find Prince William Sound, which covers over 100 miles and is the state's center for marine life, oil production, and port facilities. More than 220 species of birds, 30 species of land mammals, and at least a dozen marine mammal species are found in the region. Bald eagles are plentiful along treetops and shorelines (*Prince William Sound*, n.d.). Among the maritime species, it will be possible to see whales, otters, seals, and sea lions in credible numbers along the shore. But it is not only marine life and birds that you will find: It is also possible to see brown and black bears near the mountains and fishing for salmon in the water along the coast.

The main cities in the area are Cordova, Valdez, and Whittier, with the last two being accessible by road while all three are accessible by boat. Here, the highlight will be Valdez, which many might remember because of an oil spill that occurred there in 1989. In fact, it was the oil spill that brought many of Valdez's residents to the region since they arrived to help with the cleanup process after the disaster. The town that saw the Alaska Gold Rush between 1867 and 1910 and survived earthquake destruction in 1964 remains an entrance point for wildlife protection, exploration, and integration with the oil explorations today.

Oil transportation is done through the Trans-Alaska Pipeline System (TAPS), which was approved by the government in 1973. Today, the TAPS continues to operate for oil transportation from the north to the south of the state and to the port to fill the tankers. Despite the disaster in 1989, there have been no incidents since then with the TAPS or anything related to oil. Today, there are no signs of the disaster as it was thoroughly cleaned, and the region is flourishing, making it one of the main attractions in Prince William Sound. Tourists who visit this town of less than 4,000 people will be able to explore its history, which is shown in the local museum, and see the influence of different generations in its landscape.

WRANGELL-ST. ELIAS NATIONAL PARK: AMERICA'S LARGEST NATIONAL PARK

This park has over 13 million acres and is the same size as Yellowstone National Park, Yosemite National Park, and Switzerland combined! (National Park Service, 2024a). Visitors can see glaciers, volcanoes, watersheds, rivers, streams, and much more there. As you might imagine, all these varied landscapes shelter millions of animals, including all three types of bears in the state. Apart from the black, and brown bears, you will find moose, sheep, caribou, wolves, mountain goats, and bison.

When visiting this national park, it is only natural that you will be overwhelmed. There is so much to see and do that exploring the most attractive and main areas will often take more than three days. One option visitors can take is flying over the park to get a better view of the landscape and wildlife, allowing them to better select the areas they want to see. The information for this can be found in the Wrangell-St. Elias Visitor Center and the Kennecott Visitor Center, both of which are located at the park's entrances.

Today, the park has some cabins that can be used by the public, of which four (Viking Lodge, Caribou Creek, Nugget Creek, and Esker Stream) need to be reserved ahead of time. Other public cabins are offered on a first-come, first-served basis. Please note that these cabins do not have running water or plumbing, so there are no showers or toilets. It is a very rustic experience; you must bring your own firewood and remember the no-trace principles for its use. Camping is also possible, but it is essential to consider that there are limited areas where help and supplies can be obtained due to its remote location.

To move around the park, it is important to remember that access is limited and mostly reserved for off-road motorized vehicles. Most of the time, visitors will need to explore the park on foot due to the terrain and to interfere with the area as little as possible. Experiences within the park include rafting, mountaineering, backcountry hiking, kayaking, trekking, and wildlife viewing. To ensure the best experience, you must bring everything you will need to enjoy the trip, from food supplies to utilities, as urban areas near the park can be distant to reach.

Author's tip: The best way to visit this park is to explore it in sections. Due to its size, you can only explore a portion of it daily. The Visitor Center, located in the Copper Central Area, has maps and information about the best hiking spots and park roads.

ACCOMMODATION AND DINING OPTIONS

With so many options for places to go and things to see, you are likely wondering where the best places to stay and eat are when you visit Southcentral Alaska. In the final section of this chapter, you will get some recommendations for lodging and dining with possibilities for different budgets. In this case, $ will be used for budget-friendly places, $$ for locations with average costs, and $$$ for more expensive experiences.

Where to Stay

- Alyeska Resort (Girdwood): $$$
- Beluga Lake Lodge (Homer): $
- Best Western Valdez Harbor Inn (Valdez): $$
- Breeze Inn (Seward): $
- Coast Inn at Lake Hood (Anchorage): $$
- Grand View Inn & Suites (Wasilla): $$
- Hilton Anchorage (Anchorage): $$$
- Jewel Lake Bed and Breakfast (Anchorage): $$
- Kenai Princess Wilderness Lodge (Kenai): $$
- Land's End Resort (Homer): $
- Sheep Mountain Lodge (Glacier View): $$
- Soldotna Inn (Soldotna): $
- Talkeetna Inn (Talkeetna): $$
- The Hotel Captain Cook (Anchorage) $$
- Tutka Bay Lodge (Kachemak Bay State Park): $$

Although these are some of the traditional lodgings available, it is also possible to camp or use the public cabins as mentioned previously. Check online to see if reservations are required for fees. Additionally, remember to read the rules and regulations of each park to identify if lighting a campfire is allowed and what services and amenities are available.

Where to Dine

49th State Brewing; Anchorage; $$; Brewery—Mexican and Alaskan food

A Rogue's Garden;Valdez; $; Natural and organic

Big Swig Brewery; Anchorage;$$; Alaskan

Burger Bus; Kenai; $; Burgers made of fish and meat

China Sea; Whittier; $$; Chinese

Denali Brewing Company; Talkeetna; $$; Brewery—Hamburgers and meat

Fresh Sourdough Express Bakery; Homer; $; Baked goods

Glacier Brewhouse; Anchorage; $$; Brewery, American

La Baleine; Homer; $; Sandwiches and seafood

Le Barn Appétit; Seward; $$; French crepes

Orso; Anchorage; $$$; Alaskan–Italian

Simon & Seafort's; Anchorage; $$$; Alaskan, American & seafood

Sunrise Inn; Cooper Landing; $$; Alaskan and burgers

The Crow's Nest Restaurant; Anchorage; $$$; Alaskan–French

The Roadhouse Bakery; Talkeetna; $; Baked goods and sandwiches

The Saltry; Halibut Cove; $$; Seafood

As we continue exploring the opportunities in Alaska, it is time to move to another region. We will now move to the Southwest, where you can visit the world's salmon capital and explore two more national parks.

SOUTHWEST ALASKA

Despite not being on the state's road system, visitors wishing to explore Southwest Alaska can get to the region by plane or boat. In one of its most rustic regions, with two national parks and plenty of wildlife, this is certainly the place to go if you are interested in fishing for salmon and learning more about the industry. Home to the Alaska Native communities of the Yup'ik, Cup'ik, Unangax̂, and Sugpiaq (Alutiiq), it has some of the most traditional experiences you can find when visiting the state.

In this chapter, you will discover the region's best attractions, from wildlife viewing opportunities to cultural experiences and sports events. With its vast coast extending from the Cook Inlet to the Bering Sea and beautiful landscapes including glaciers, mountains, volcanoes, and lakes, there are more than enough picture-perfect moments to enjoy. Read on to discover all that Southwest Alaska offers and prepare for the adventure of a lifetime!

BETHEL: GATEWAY TO THE YUKON-KUSKOKWIM DELTA

When visiting Southwest Alaska, the town of Bethel will likely be planned into the trip. This is because the community is the largest in the Yukon-Kuskokwim Delta. It serves as the port of entrance for the supplies for all the other villages around it. Despite having a population of almost 6,500, it is still considered a rural community and the largest in the state. Most of its residents are Alaska Native and live on subsistence and craft items for commercialization and personal use. Due to the limited access to supplies, the prices can be rather high, although they are still cheaper than in smaller villages.

Although no state roads lead into the town, there are daily flights from Anchorage to the city, sometimes more than three times daily. Once there, you can catch a taxi, the most popular form of transportation. In many cases, this experience can lead you to share a cab with another passenger, usually another traveler or a Native, allowing you to meet different people as soon as you arrive or as you move around the town.

While in Bethel and visiting its surrounding area, you will have the perfect opportunity to immerse yourself in the Alaska Native culture since most of its inhabitants are Yup'ik

Eskimo and still speak their traditional language. One of the best places to do this is the Yupiit Piciryarait Cultural Center, which is in the same building as the University of Alaska and the Regional Cultural Center. There, you can see expositions on local household items, traditional toys, and other objects pertaining to the Natives' culture.

As you might imagine, one of the town's main attractions that leads into the Yukon-Kuskokwim Delta is wildlife observation, with a special mention of birdwatching. Nearby, it is possible to visit the Yukon Delta National Wildlife Refuge, where you can participate in a guided tour showing you some of the region's native species that visit, especially during the summer. As an added benefit, while in town, you can also walk at the end of the day on the local boardwalk, participate in socialization with the locals, and even get the chance to learn more from an elder.

Author's tip: Guided tours are the best way to increase your chances of spotting wildlife. The tour guides are usually accompanied by a certified biologist who can point out and identify species you will see during your trip. There are so many different animals and birds in the area, but it is never guaranteed what you will see (Meeuwesen, 2020).

DILLINGHAM: SALMON CAPITAL OF THE WORLD

The town of Dillingham, known as the Salmon Capital of the world, attracts thousands of visitors every summer looking to sport fish and taste some of its delicious products. Here, those looking to catch some fish will find all varieties of salmon available in the state, as well as rainbow trout, making it not only a fun adventure but also a tasty one. Dillingham has a little over 2,000 residents and is located at the margins of the Nushagak and Wood Rivers in the center of Nushagak Bay.

Near the small town, visitors will find the opportunity to see a unique place: the Walrus Islands State Game Sanctuary. This spot is particularly popular with those who want to see marine wildlife. It will be possible to see the largest walrus haul-out grounds in Alaska, where each summer as many as 14,000 male walruses haul out on exposed, rocky beaches to stake out their territory for the upcoming mating season (*Dillingham*, n.d.). But this is only a small part of what you can see.

The greatest attraction in the Dillingham region for wildlife lovers is the Togiak National Wildlife Refuge, established in 1980 and home to the Ahklun Mountains, which occupy most of its extension. Due to its several water sources, there is an abundance of fish, which provide the local community with the food they need year-round. The area is highly preserved, including by the Alaska National Interest Lands Conservation Act, which means that only noninvasive recreational activities can be carried out.

Author's tip: Depending on where you want to enter the Togiak National Wildlife Refuge, you will need to catch a bush plane from either Gillingham or Bethel. The general office is in Dillingham, but if you want to enter through the northeast, the best option is to leave from Bethel since access to the Kanektok River will be faster and easier.

LAKE CLARK NATIONAL PARK AND PRESERVE: UNTAMED WILDERNESS

With over four million acres in area and home to the ancestral Dena'ina people, this national park offers some of the most magnificent landscapes of forestry, water, and mountains in one place. Lake Clark is located in the center of the park and is the destination for many people who want to engage in water-based activities such as kayaking and swimming. At the same time, the different rivers and lakes throughout the park offer the perfect opportunity to refresh and cool down during the summer or even catch some fish, which are abundant in the park.

At the same time, those wishing to catch a glimpse of the local wildlife will find ample opportunity here. You can see brown bears, moose, sheep, and birds as you hike through one of its many trails. There are trails in the park suitable for all types of abilities, with short, easy hikes and longer, more challenging ones. If you want to have a better overview of the park, there are third-party companies that offer flying tours, taking visitors exactly to the places where these animals can be found while providing the perfect opportunity to see its amazing landscape from above.

If you plan to stay in the park, you can stay in one of its lodges or public cabins. These cabins must be reserved in advance. They are rustic, with no plumbing, electricity, or running water. This means you must bring your own supplies, bedding, towels, and silverware to enjoy your stay. Port Alsworth, Upper Twin Lake, Silver Salmon Creek, and Crescent Lake offer different accommodation options.

Author's tip: To select the best lodging for you and your group, look at the park's map and identify the region you want to explore. Due to the limited transportation possibilities within the park, establishing the region you want to visit the most and finding relevant accommodation near that area will be essential to save time and give you the best opportunity to enjoy your visit.

KING SALMON: GATEWAY TO KATMAI AND BRISTOL BAY

Located on the banks of the Naknek River, King Salmon is the perfect place to establish a base when visiting the region.

If you are interested in sport fishing and practicing outdoor activities, this will be the perfect place to stay, especially due to its proximity to Katmai National Park. The most common way to visit this area is to choose a travel package tailored to your needs and wants and optimize the experience. In many cases, transportation, food, and lodging will be included, leaving you the job of enjoying the trip.

The area is known for having all five species of salmon in Alaska available and offering those who visit an amazing culinary experience in some of its restaurants. The best time of the year to visit the region for fishing is from early June to late September. Many of the towns' populations double during the summer months with the number of anglers who are working for the large fishing companies in Bristol Bay.

King Salmon will also be the best place to set up camp for those who want to explore Katmai National Park and plan on watching wildlife while they are in the region. The town is just a short distance from the park, and several tours and excursions leave from it for those interested in having a guided experience. At the same time, if you want to see other wildlife, it also offers access to numerous fly-in fishing and adventure camps and lodges on the Alaska Peninsula as well as wildlife viewing expeditions in Becharof National Wildlife Refuge, the Alaska Peninsula National Wildlife Refuge, and McNeil River State Game Sanctuary (*King Salmon*, n.d.).

KATMAI NATIONAL PARK AND PRESERVE: LAND OF THE GIANTS

If your objective for visiting Alaska is bear-viewing, then Katmai National Park is the must-see place for your vacation. World-renowned for its bear population, which surpasses 2,000, going to this park will almost ensure that you will see them in their natural habitat. For the best opportunities to view them, go to Brooks Falls, where you will likely see them fishing for salmon through June to August. Several companies offer fly-in one-day and extended trips to the park from Anchorage and King Salmon, which is the ideal way to reach the area.

Although bears are the highlight of visiting the park, another of its significant features is the Valley of 10,000 Smokes Road, the only one in the park that will offer you incomparable views of the area shaped by a volcano eruption in 1912. The valley is a product of the 20th century's largest volcanic eruption, makes for incredible walking, the mandatory elevation gain is minimal, and the views cannot be beaten

(*The Valley of 10,000 Smokes*, n.d.). Once there, you can choose between different hiking options and adventures.

For those interested in obtaining a guided hiking tour of the park, these are available and led by park rangers and leave from Brooks Camp. Other tours are available from different service providers, and your choice will depend on the budget and time you have available for the trip. If you stay for more than one day, finding lodging and camping sites near Brooks Camp or staying in King Salmon for better access is possible. Lodging at Brooks Camp is available from June 1 until September 17. Reservations are necessary. They also offer guided sport fishing, gifts, merchandise, recreation equipment rentals, showers, ground transportation, sight-seeing, and camper drop-off services (National Park Service, 2023).

Author's tip: Water is scarce in the Valley of 10,000 Smokes, so bring plenty. If you wear contact lenses, wearing a pair of goggles or glasses is also important since the region can be quite windy, bringing discomfort for those with contacts.

KODIAK ISLAND: THE EMERALD ISLE

Located southwest of Anchorage and only reachable by flight or boat, the largest island belonging to Alaska is also one of its main attractions. Here, the superstars are not the different animal species you will find—these are few—instead, you will find several thousand Kodiak bears, a unique subspecies of the traditional brown bear that have adapted to the island. A large male Kodiak bear might stand five feet high at the shoulder while still on all fours. On hind legs, it can reach 10 feet tall. And Kodiak has more brown bears per square mile than virtually anywhere (*Kodiak Island*, n.d.).

While bears are the island's main attraction, you can observe other wildlife while you visit. These animals include bison, weasels, mountain goats, reindeer, beavers, and deer. The variety of marine wildlife that can be observed from the coast or boat is also vast. These include sea lions, whales, sea otters, and porpoises.

Ideally speaking, visitors should stay at least two nights on the island to explore all the things it has to offer, such as a Russian Orthodox Church, the Alutiiq Museum, Pyramid Peak, hundreds of miles of trails for hiking, and many historic places that were left after World War II. Within the small town, there are a few options for formal lodging in cabins and hotels, or you can take your gear and camp in the Fort Abercrombie State Park. You will also find a few restaurants and dining options serving approximately 5,000 people and tourists.

Author's tip: Although there are over 3,500 bears on the island, viewing them might not be so obvious since they are located in the remote Kodiak National Wildlife Refuge, with no roads. To see these animals, visitors will ideally have to book a flightseeing tour or engage in an excursion on foot through the area. Depending on the season, some observation tours can be expensive, so it is best to check the prices first if you are traveling on a budget.

ALEUTIAN ISLANDS: CHAIN OF VOLCANIC WONDER

This archipelago, made of over 200 islands, is located at the extreme west of the state and extends over 1,200 miles. Its most distinctive feature is that these islands are made of 57 volcano peaks at the north extremity of the Pacific Ring of Fire. Of these almost 60 volcanoes, 27 are active and have erupted in the past 250 years. Despite its remote location and challenging conditions, it is home to 8,000 Alaska Natives, mostly those from the Unangax̂ community, known today as Aleut.

The Russians first occupied these islands, who still own some of them near their territory. They are the barrier between the Pacific Ocean and the North Sea, close to the Bering Strait. After being occupied by the Russians and bought by the Americans in 1867 with the remainder of the state, it was later occupied during World War II by the Japanese. Due to its strategic location, military personnel previously occupied it, especially during the Cold War, but this is no longer the region's reality. Today, many visitors can see structures that have remained for all three periods and are a part of Aleutian history.

Because of its characteristics, the wildlife in the region is so different from others in the state. Although mammals have been introduced to the islands by humans, the native animals consist of only birds and sea animals. While the former can still be observed today in many species, especially during the summer, the latter has significantly decreased due to human predatory practices. Marine mammals include the endangered Steller sea lion, threatened northern sea otter, and harbor seal. The principal marine fish are halibut, cod, rockfish, sablefish, yellowfin sole, pollack, sand lance, herring, and salmon (*Aleutian Islands Wilderness*, 2018).

Apart from wildlife observation, another popular activity on the islands is hiking, with thousands of trail miles that can be explored in unparalleled beauty. On these trails, you can explore volcanoes covered in snow and green foliage mostly untouched by humans. From the higher areas, you can see the agitated sea waves crashing onto the rocks. These characteristics make entering the water and engaging in sports extremely dangerous.

As for the developed areas, there are four significant towns, with a special mention for Unalaska, the home to the Port of Dutch Harbor and where over half of the population resides. This is one of the only airports on the islands, and getting there takes approximately three hours by plane or three days by cruise. For those looking to explore the rugged coast or even explore the secrets of the region, specialized companies carry out guided week-long tours with an all-inclusive package.

If you visit independently, you will want to find accommodation in Unalaska, which can be pricey due to the region's limitations. However, you will also find different museums, historic buildings, and abandoned WWII structures there to visit. Despite its remote locale, Unalaska offers fine dining restaurants, a hotel, a full-service community center, pool, library, nationally awarded schools, museums, local festivals, and sporting events, and more, weave this tight-knit community together in extraordinary ways (*Unalaska*, n.d.).

Author's tip: One of the must-see attractions of the Aleutian Islands is the Port of Dutch Harbor in Unalaska. Today, the port is considered one of the most important for fishing products in the world, the first in the U.S. It transports millions of dollars in products every season to supply the mainland and other countries with salmon and cod. Depending on the season you visit, you will see the fishers at work as they bring in their catch of the day.

ACCOMMODATIONS AND DINING

Despite being a more remote location compared to other Alaskan regions, you will discover several accommodations and dining options in Southwest Alaska. However, it is significantly more expensive here compared to more populated areas because of the previously mentioned difficulty in obtaining supplies. Although these are more formal settings, it is also possible to find alternatives for lodging, including Airbnb places for rent and even rooms and smaller local restaurants you can't find online. If you plan on visiting this region, remember to reserve in advance due to the high influx of people during the summer.

Accommodation

Here are some options for lodging in the Southwest region of Alaska and the town it can be found in:

- 9th Wave Bed and Breakfast (Chiniak): $$

- Bear Paw Inn (Dillingham): $$
- Best Western Kodiak Inn (Kodiak): $$
- Bristol Bay Lodge (Dillingham): $$$
- Cranky Crow Bed and Breakfast (Kodiak): $$
- Crystal Creek Lodge (King Salmon): $$$
- Katmai Lodge (King Salmon): $$$
- Mission Lodge (Lake Aleknagik): $$$
- Grand Aleutian Hotel (Unalaska): $$$
- Quality Inn Kodiak (Women's Bay): $$

As usual, campsites and public cabins are available inside each park in addition to these lodging opportunities. If you want to stay in either of these, it is essential to check with the National Park's information service to see if reservations are required and if there is a cost. While many of these areas will be on a first-come, first-served basis, checking to be sure will help you plan in advance.

Dining

As you might imagine, the main attraction of the region's restaurants is the fish-based dishes. Here, you will also likely find more food that is cooked by Alaska Natives, including traditional dishes that are not found anywhere else. Here are a few options you might want to explore and their details.

Name; Location; Price; Cuisine

Bayside Diner; Dillingham; $$; American

D&D Restaurant; Nanek; $$; Pizza and American

El Chicano; Kodiak; $$; Mexican

Kito's Kave; King Salmon; $$; Seafood

Kodiak Hana; Kodiak; $$; Sushi

Sockeye Saloon; King Salmon; $; Bar and grill

The Chart Room; Unalaska; $$$; Seafood

Unisea; Unalaska; $$; Seafood

Now that we have explored the state's west, it is time to move to the opposite end, the region located east of Anchorage. Also known as Southeast Alaska, the state's capital, Juneau, is located here. With a vibrant community, traditions, wildlife, and other national parks to explore, you will see why this is such a popular destination for tourists and locals alike. Read on to discover Alaskan history, explore outdoor wonders, engage in scenic rides, and enjoy the icy landscapes of Alaska.

SOUTHEAST ALASKA

> *The grand show is eternal. It is always sunrise some-*
> *where; the dew is never all dried at once; a shower is*
> *forever falling; vapor ever rising. Eternal sunrise,*
> *eternal sunset, eternal dawn and gloaming, on sea*
> *and continents and islands, each in its turn, as the*
> *round earth rolls.*
>
> — JOHN MUIR

It is only natural that many Alaska visitors choose to explore one of its most beautiful and important cities: Juneau. The city, located in Southeast Alaska, is the state's capital and, similarly to other locations, offers different cultural and outdoor experiences to those you might have visited. However, as you are about to learn, there is much more to this region than just Juneau. There are other experiences here that will be just as breathtaking as others in the state.

In this chapter, you will discover the heart of Southeast Alaska and all it has to offer those visiting. With incredible opportunities to learn about the history and enjoy the local cuisine, it is possible to enjoy the urban and outdoor experience all in one here. As you explore these outdoor wonders, engage in scenic rides, and enjoy the icy landscapes of Alaska, you will never want to leave!

JUNEAU: ALASKA'S CAPITAL CITY

Although Juneau is the state capital, its small-town feel embraces visitors. Downtown Juneau, which can be explored on foot, offers different restaurants, shops, and art galleries with pieces made by local artists. Founded in the 1880s and named the state capital in 1906, it is one of the least accessible state capitals in the U.S. due to its location.

Nestled between mountains and the ocean, it is the only state capital in the country accessible only by boat or plane. Its population is just over 30,000, a home to administrators, tech wizards, artists, wildlife-watchers and adventurers, who, together, have helped to forge a laidback city with a close-to-nature feel (Gregg, 2023). One of the city's main tourist attractions is that while the climate is milder here compared to the other regions in Alaska, it still offers similar experiences, including wildlife viewing of bears and whales, outdoor sports, and fishing.

As you explore the capital, you can see different architectural styles, mixing the old with the new. It is in this area that the State Capitol Building stands out. Built in 1931, visitors can explore some of Alaska's history and way of life, depicted on murals. Visitors are welcome to explore more of the building in self-guided weekday tours during business hours. Other buildings worth seeing include the Alaska State Museum, the Juneau Douglas City Museum, and the Sealaska Heritage Institute.

For those looking for outdoor experiences, the Tongass National Forest is the best place to participate in recreational activities surrounded by nature. The park has a diversified landscape, with snow and ice, green areas, lakes, waterfalls, and much more. Here, there is a chance of seeing bears, wolves, deer, sea otters and seals. For those interested in an even more in-depth experience, the Tongass National Forest offers over 20 campsites within the forest and other designated areas and several possibilities for backcountry camping.

Author's tip: If possible and within budget, you should book a cruise tour leaving the Port of Juneau. From this, it is possible to explore the nearby regional glaciers and watch whales and other marine animals. One of the most famous cruise routes in the area is to the Tracy-Arm fjord, 50 miles southeast of Juneau, with a pair of tidewater glaciers that shed icebergs into the fjord's deep waters. You're almost guaranteed to see seals inside the arm, and you might also spot humpbacks, orcas, and eagles (*Juneau*, n.d.). Prices for these guided tours usually start at $150 per person for an approximate 4-hour navigation experience.

SKAGWAY: GATEWAY TO THE KLONDIKE

Skagway is one of Alaska's many small towns with incredible historic significance. It was established at the end of the 1800s, during the Klondike Gold Rush in the state, and it is still possible to see reminiscences of the period as you visit. For those establishing Juneau as their base for their Alaska experience, it is the perfect destination for a day trip to learn about the gold rush in the region and explore the land that includes lakes and mountains.

Although the town's population is less than 1,000, it offers great opportunities to visit one of the old saloons that miners and other locals frequented during the gold rush. At the time of what became known as the Klondike Gold Rush, the town's population reached upward of 10,000. Still, as gold became scarcer over time, the population slowly dropped to what it is today. The American government established the Klondike Gold Rush National Park in 1976, which preserves most of the mining facilities and landscape of the time.

Today, the park receives thousands of visitors annually to hike the Chilkoot trail, which extends for 33 miles and shows artifacts and constructions left by the miners from the time. This was a frequent route for the miners who opted for the cheapest and most direct routes to the Yukon River, an area where gold was found, along with the White Pass trail. Another of the park's attractions is the ghost townsite of Dyea. Visitors who want to explore the area should check the NPS page for the park before going since the Chilkoot trail frequently undergoes maintenance due to the constant floods that damage the area.

Almost one million tourists visit this national park today, looking to explore the historic sites, public buildings, and outdoor experiences it offers. Due to its proximity to Juneau (95 miles), it is the perfect place to spend the day or even a night in one of its 22 campgrounds. Skagway is reachable by car, plane, or bus, with different companies offering the service and departing from the capital.

Author's tip: For visitors who want to explore the region in more detail, you catch a train in Skagway that will take you through the White Pass Summit and different landscapes in the region. The tour takes approximately 2.5 hours, and it will be possible to see the Yukon River, the Sawtooth Range, and the Dead Horse Gulch. Visitors will find that it is possible to book in the morning, available daily, for the soft morning light, or an evening train, which runs Tuesdays, Wednesdays, and Thursdays, for the glow of the evening light. There are also fewer passengers on these trains (*White Pass & Yukon Route Railroad*, n.d.).

HAINES: ADVENTURE IN THE CHILKAT VALLEY

The small town of Haines is just a 45-minute ferry ride from Skagway. Despite its small population of just over 2,000, it becomes a paradise in the summer for those looking for adventures. Here, it is possible to engage in outdoor sports and activities, observe wildlife, and walk through the town's picturesque downtown, which has a well-preserved history from the Klondike Gold Rush. Not by chance, most people who travel toward the town seek a peaceful environment away from the busy urban centers.

One of the most popular attractions in the region is rafting through the Alaska Chilkat Bald Eagle Reserve, where it is possible to see thousands of birds building their nests or resting in trees during September to December. For those who admire these regal animals, visiting the reserve is a must to observe their habits, watch them fishing salmon in the water, and take that perfect photograph. If you plan on visiting the area, it is essential to learn the rules you need to follow to avoid stressing the birds, getting lost, or bumping into other enthusiasts.

On the other hand, if you are looking for something with more adrenaline, you will want to take advantage of the sports adventures in the area. Apart from rafting and fishing, it is also possible to go kayaking, hiking, and biking in the region. Those who have extra in their budget and are visiting during the winter might want to use this opportunity to go heli-hiking, which leaves the hikers in a region only accessible by helicopter. For all outdoor activities on land, air, or water, taking guided tours with specialized guides is possible to ensure you have the best experience available. These can be bought in Skagway or Haines, with a starting price of $250.

KETCHIKAN: SALMON CAPITAL OF THE WORLD

In the southernmost city of Alaska, thousands of fishermen gather every summer for the opportunity to catch one of the five salmon species that inhabit the region. In Ketchikan, it is possible to see the one-in-a-lifetime experience at the Ketchikan Creek Falls of watching the fish trying to travel upstream looking for calmer water. Due to the incredible number of fish in the region, Ketchikan is known as the salmon capital of the world, attracting many first-timers and experienced anglers to one of its popular fishing cruises.

With just over 8,000 people, walking through calm streets during the other seasons of the year is possible. Additionally, due to its fishing industry, restaurants usually serve fresh salmon, which is a delight for those who love it. Although fishing is the main attraction in Ketchikan, the town has one other significant cultural feature: totem poles from the Alaska Native Tlingit people.

Dating back hundreds of years, totem poles were created as a way to represent their history, traditions, life and death, familial lineage, success, thanks and remembrance, story-telling, and local animals. The Totem Heritage Center, where these totem poles are located, has the largest collection of unrestored 19th-century totem poles, but that's just the beginning of what it has to offer! Also displayed are baskets, masks, regalia, carvings, and the incredible photographs of the old villages (*Totem Heritage Center*, n.d.). This unforget-table experience starts outside the center, where you can see different totems. Inside, it is possible to see totems older than 150 years old and removed with guidance made by the Native elders, who also used the opportunity to talk about its history and symbology.

SITKA: WHERE RUSSIA MEETS ALASKA

This town of a little over 9,000 inhabitants was once the capital of Russia, Alaska, until the state was bought by the U.S. Today, it is still possible to see the Russian influence in the town, especially in its construction. The two most popular buildings are the St. Michael's Cathedral and the Russian Bishop's House, built in the mid-1800s and still preserved. The cathedral was still a significant landmark in the state by the early 1900s. It was built in the style of tradi-tional Russian architecture. Although its original structure was destroyed by a fire in 1966, most of its artifacts and valuables were rescued by the locals. This can be seen in a tour of the building, which is also a working church.

Although it has a significant history, Sitka is also one of the best places in Southeast Alaska to see bears, especially due to the Fortress of the Bear Rescue Center, which cares for orphaned brown and black cubs. At the same time, as the only city in the region located on the coast, it will provide incredible opportunities to see sea otters, whales, and other marine animals. To get a good view of them, take a cruise from the port or rent a kayak or canoe to explore on your own.

For an even richer outdoor experience, visitors can visit the Sitka National Historical Park, which is responsible for preserving the battle site between the Russians when they first arrived and the Native Tlingit. There, it is possible to see dozens of beautiful totem poles sculpted by the Alaska Natives and visit the Russian bishop's house, which still holds the original dishes and furniture from the time. The park is perfect for a day trip (no camping allowed) and learning more about the historical occupation. From there, it is possible to find restaurants and accommodations within walking distance.

Finally, there is the unmissable Sitka Sound Science Center for wildlife lovers who want to learn about the town's efforts to preserve marine species specifically. The center was formed in 2007 and comprises a salmon hatchery, an aquarium, research lab and an education outreach that encompasses preschoolers to college students and lifelong learners of all ages (*Sitka Sound Science Center*, n.d.). There are activities for children and adults, including a 30-minute tour of the installation with a knowledgeable guide. During the summer, tours are offered more than once a day, and educational programs are open to the community by paying an admission fee.

GLACIER BAY NATIONAL PARK AND PRESERVE: ICE AND WILDLIFE

In the only national park located in Southeast Alaska, what you can see in Glacier Bay National Park might be given away by its name. However, the park is much more than the opportunity to see magnificent glaciers up close—you will also have the chance to hike within its forests and fjords and navigate its tidewater glaciers. As with many other state parks, the only way to reach Glacier Bay is by plane or boat, the latter being more common since it also offers the opportunity to see the different marine species along the way.

One of the distinguishing characteristics of this national park is that, when silent, it is possible to hear the sounds it makes. These include singing birds, glaciers crashing and whistling, and the sea lions calling. In fact, this park feature is so important that the NPS has a program named "Voices of Glacier Bay Soundscape Project," where it is possible to listen to its different sounds on the official webpage. According to the National Park Service (2022), "Glacier Bay may be the premier location for Alaska's heritage of wild sounds. In order to fully understand and protect this heritage, we must start by recording how these places sound today."

For those who want to stay in the park for more than one day, there are several lodging opportunities inside and outside the park. Within the park are the Glacier Bay Lodge and the Bartlett Cove Campground, and nearby is the town of Gustavus, which also offers different lodging opportunities just nine miles away. Both in Bartlett Cove, where the park's headquarters is located, and in Gustavus, it is possible to rent gear for hiking, kayaking, fishing, and camping or enlist to participate in one of the mountaineering sea expeditions carried out by contractors.

Author's tip: If you are interested in visiting the Glacier Bay National Park for marine wildlife and glacier watching, you do not necessarily need to disembark from the cruise you are taking. In fact, most visitors who go to the park by cruise ship can use the experience to see the best of what the park has to offer. Some expeditions leave from more distant regions and will take tourists on a round day trip that will allow them to set up base in less remote areas.

PETERSBURG: LITTLE NORWAY

Petersburg was settled in the 19th century when Norwegian Peter Buschmann arrived and started working on building the town. The town's name was given in his honor, and soon, many from Scandinavia were arriving to join Peter in the new settlement that became known as "Little Norway." Due to the large number of immigrants, the traditions were kept, and today, much of this influence by European countries can be seen in their food and traditions.

Apart from European architecture, one of the most significant markers was the establishment of the Sons of Norway Lodge, built on one of the piers that holds the traditions of the Scandinavian community in the area. While strolling through downtown Petersburg, observing urban art and local creations in many art galleries and museums is possible. Today, the region is known for its fish canning industry, with millions of pounds produced every year. The number of fish in the area is also an amazing opportunity for those who want to try. You can catch fish that weigh up to 300 pounds.

One of the best opportunities for visitors to enjoy the local culture is during the third week of May, when the Little Norway Festival is held annually to celebrate the people's heritage. The date is not a coincidence—it was chosen to coincide with the signing of Norway's Constitution in 1814. During the fest, it is possible to see people dressed as Vikings and Valkyries, eat traditional Norwegian dishes, listen to music and watch shows, and participate in a pageant or a walk-or-run race.

WRANGELL: ISLAND HISTORY AND CULTURE

Wrangell is located on an island of the same name in the southeastern part of the state in the middle of the Alexander Archipelago. This small town has a population of roughly 2,000 inhabitants and is mostly surrounded by green areas, glaciers, and water. Before the arrival of the English, the Alaska Native community of the Tlingit people used to live there, marking the landscape with symbols that can still be seen today.

One is Petroglyph Beach, where over 40 primitive artistic expressions have been identified. Many of these drawings show animals, faces, and symbols. There is some belief that the petroglyphs pre-date the Tlingit Indians of this area, one of the factors that make the meanings of the etchings inscrutable (*Petroglyph Beach*, n.d.). Due to tourists' interest in the historic petroglyphs, replicas are spread through the city's walkway so people can touch them. The beach is currently protected and can only be accessed by a boardwalk and deck.

From this boardwalk, visitors can also cross the Stikine River, one of the area's largest rivers, extending for almost 340 miles. Its relevance is not only to the natural landscape and the wildlife it harbors, but it was also an essential access route to the Klondike area during the gold rush. Today, many people visit it to see the canyon that has been sculpted by the water and the integration of the waters with the forests and tundra. Among the wildlife that lives in the area, it is possible to see birds, beavers, moose, otters, and, of course, bears. Most of the wildlife becomes more visible during spring and summer when the weather is hotter and the snow is melting, offering more opportunities for food.

ACCOMMODATION AND DINING

Depending on when you start looking, finding a place to stay in Southeast Alaska may be challenging. The same can be said for some dining possibilities during the high season. Visitors must often make reservations or wait in line to sit and eat. If you are more adventurous and want to enjoy the outdoors, grab a sandwich or a bite and eat on the benches that line the street or alongside the water during the day. In this section, we will explore the different options for accommodations and dining in the region, and estimated price ranges are once again represented by $, $$, and $$$.

Accommodations

As you look for places to stay in the Southeast region, you will notice options for all types of budgets. From basic hostels to fancier five-star hotels, booking accommodation that fits your needs is possible. However, as with the rest of the state, you must book in advance because it is likely that everything will be at full occupancy starting in mid-April. If you want to take advantage of the opportunity to select the option that best fits your needs, you should start planning as soon as possible! Here are some of the options for staying in Southeast Alaska:

- Alaska's Capital Inn Bed and Breakfast (Juneau): $
- Alaskan Hotel and Bar (Juneau): $
- Aspen Suites Hotel Haines (Haines): $$$
- Baranor Downtown, B.W. Signature Collection (Juneau): $$$
- Eagle Bay Inn (Sitka): $$
- Four Points by Sheraton Juneau (Juneau): $$$
- Gustavus Bay Lodge (Gustavus): $$
- Icy Strait Lodge (Hoonah): $$
- My Place Hotel (Ketchikan): $$
- Scandia House Hotel (Petersburg): $$
- Silverbow Inn Hotel & Suites (Juneau): $$$
- Sitka Hotel and Restaurant (Sitka): $$$
- The Cape Fox Lodge (Ketchikan): $$
- The Ketchikan Hostel (Ketchikan): $
- The Landing Hotel and Restaurant (Ketchikan): $$

It is always important to remember that the ideal solution is to set up a base in a specific city and travel by ferry or cruise to other places you want to explore. There will be opportunities to camp in designated areas and even in the backcountry in many parks. However, in most cases, reservations can't be made, and visitors must try their luck on a first-come, first-served basis. For Glacier Bay National Park, the lodge is an option, and you will want to call them beforehand to check availability.

Dining

You will find many cuisines when looking for dining opportunities in Southeast Alaska. Although most of the local dishes are based on seafood, there are other specialties you can find as you navigate through the different cities. Juneau and Ketchikan are the two cities with the highest number of restaurants specializing in seafood. Nonetheless, you will also be able to find Mexican, Italian, Asian, and even Russian specialties in some of the most popular dining spaces. Let's check them out!

Name; Location; Price; Cuisine

Alaska Brewing Company; Juneau; $$; Brewery and seafood

Bar Harbor Restaurant; Ketchikan; $$; American and seafood

Bombay Curry; Skagway; $$$; Indian

Coastal Cold Storage; Petersburg; $; Seafood

Excursion Restaurant; Gustavus; $$$; Seafood

Island Pub; Juneau; $$; Pizza and bar

Ludvig's Bistro; Sitka; $$$; Seafood

Michelle's Taste of Asia; Ketchikan; $$; Asian

Ocean View Restaurante; Ketchikan; $$; Italian–Mexican

Pel Meni; Juneau; $; Russian

Salt; Juneau; $$$; Seafood

Stikine Inn; Wrangell; $$$; Seafood

Sweet Mermaids; Ketchikan; $; Small bites and snacks

The Asylum Bar; Ketchikan; $; American

Twisted Fish; Juneau; $; Seafood

We have now examined the southern regions of Alaska, and it is time to move up north to the state's Interior, the fourth region. With its center established in Fairbanks, you will learn all about what there is to see in it and its surrounding areas. This region holds one of the state's main attractions for kids, directly connected to a famous festivity that is held annually.

INTERIOR ALASKA

> *The soul of Alaska lies in its wilderness—the vast stretches of mountain peaks, endless forests, wide rivers, and deep blue ocean harboring a tremendous diversity of wildlife.*

— GARY SNYDER

The Interior region of Alaska is the gateway to the state's vast wilderness. By setting up a base in Fairbanks, the main city in the region, visitors can explore some of the most remote areas and extraordinary landscapes. Interior Alaska occupies almost 30% of the state. It offers much to those willing to leave their comfort zone and explore all its attractions.

In this chapter, you will learn about the outdoor activities offered in the region, such as dog mushing, soaking in natural hot springs, and experiencing riverfront adventures in Nenana. Just a short ride from Fairbanks, you can see glaciers, bears, and even the North Pole (well, not the actual North Pole...)

FAIRBANKS: GATEWAY TO THE INTERIOR

Fairbanks is Alaska's second-most populated city, with approximately 100,000 inhabitants, after Anchorage. Due to its central location, with the Arctic area to the north and Anchorage to the south, it is one of the best places to explore more than one of the state's regions. The city is served by a railroad system that comes and goes to Anchorage through Denali National Park and has an international airport that you can easily fly in and out of.

For those who prefer a city setting, exploring downtown on foot and one of its many museums dedicated to the local history and traditions is possible. Downtown is the perfect place to go shopping, eat local food, and observe the architecture of historical buildings. One of its attractions is Pioneer Park, a historical theme park with plenty of rides, restaurants, relics, and museums that the whole family can enjoy. Another must-visit location is the University of Alaska Fairbanks. On a clear day, visitors can see Denali from the Alaska Range viewpoint on campus, which includes an interpretive display describing the mountainous horizon. Guided campus tours are available on most weekdays (*Fairbanks*, n.d.).

Just a short walk from downtown, you will find another of the city's main attractions: The Fairbanks Ice Museum. This place will leave you in awe of all the sculptures made with ice. The museum offers a 45-minute tour through some of the most spectacular ice sculptures artists make worldwide.

If you plan to visit during the winter, you will discover that Fairbanks and its surrounding region are close to what many would consider a snow-sports paradise. Here, it is possible to engage in activities such as skiing, dog mushing, snowboarding, backcountry skiing, ice fishing, snowshoeing, sledding, ice skating, and much more. Those interested in these sports can hire specialized tour services to take them to the best locations at prices starting at $100. Some prefer going to Fairbanks to watch the northern lights or the *aurora borealis*, a magnificent show of what nature can do.

NORTH POLE: A CHRISTMAS-THEMED EXPERIENCE

If you love the holiday season and all the feelings it brings, you will enjoy visiting North Pole. We are not talking about the actual North Pole. North Pole, for our purposes, is a small town of approximately 2,000 inhabitants located just a 20-minute drive from Fairbanks. It has everything that Christmas lovers could possibly want. You will see streets with iconic names, visit Santa's house all year, and even spend a night in the Hotel North Pole, where staying in the Santa Suite is possible. Visiting Santa's workshop is an incredible opportunity for children and adults alike to see unique toys and letters from children worldwide and eat some of Santa's favorite treats.

The town's history is unique: It was originally named Davies, but after parcels of land were bought by two entrepreneurs, the name was changed to attract more business. They had an idea of bringing a toy factory to the region, and they would then be able to advertise that all of the toys made there were made in the North Pole (*Community*, n.d.). Unfortunately, this idea did not succeed, and the toy factory never came to fruition. Other efforts have been made in the region to build a Christmas-themed attraction park, but although there is much speculation, there are still no plans for its development.

Although the town's main attraction is its unique decorations and theme, this does not mean there aren't opportunities for other activities. While visiting, it is common to see polar bears and other wildlife inhabiting the region's nearby wilderness and a group of reindeer outside Santa's house. The North Pole is also home to the Christmas in Ice exhibit, where artists from all over the world come to the town in late November to participate in the competition.

Author's tip: As you might imagine, Christmas is the most festive season for the small town. It is also when it is busiest, and volunteers work around the clock to receive tourists who come to see how the town is decorated. If you are in the region after Thanksgiving until early January, you can see the unique decorations and visit Santa himself!

CHENA HOT SPRINGS: RELAXATION AND NORTHERN LIGHTS

Chena Hot Springs is the perfect destination for those wanting to stay warm during the colder seasons. This privately owned area has an outdoor lake with hot water (approximately 160–165 °F) perfect for family enjoyment. The area, located 56 miles from Fairbanks, offers visitors a magnificent scenic drive while getting there, with plenty of open areas and wildlife to see.

Once there, apart from diving to the lake, it is possible to hike, camp, fish, and stay a night in the Chena Hot Spring Resort. For those who wish to see the Northern Lights more clearly, this is one of the best places near Fairbanks since there are no city lights to interfere. The resort also offers visitors the possibility of a day pass to experience the pool, enjoy the lights, and visit the ice museum, which is open throughout the year. For those who wish to do this, a shuttle service costs approximately $100 per person leaving and returning to Fairbanks.

For those interested in the tour, visitors will leave Fairbanks around 5 p.m. and stay in the area until 4 a.m. so they can see the lights. The tour includes indoor and outdoor pool use, so make sure you bring your swimsuit and a towel with you. You can also go by car if you want. This would allow you to arrive earlier and hike through some of the trails. For those staying in the resort, a package is offered from August to April, which includes entrances to the Aurora Ice Museum and the Northern Lights experience.

NENANA: RIVERFRONT ADVENTURES

With just over 300 residents, this small town used to be a camp for workers building the Alaska Railroad. It was visited by President Warren G. Harding, who added the final spike to the railway during its construction in 1923 (*Nenana*, n.d.).

The Nenana Depot is still standing today. It was built in 1922 and used to store the supplies for the railroad construction. It has remained important to the community ever since and now serves as the Alaska State Railroad Museum and hosts several of the community's events.

Visitors can enjoy the peace and quiet of the small-town atmosphere while engaging in fishing and other water activities. This is because Nenana is located right on the river of the calm Tanana River, which freezes during the winter. In fact, it is because of the Tanana River that its most symbolic event happens every year: the Nenana Ice Classic.

The popular contest began in 1917 when Alaska Railroad surveyors pooled $800 and bet on when the ice would disintegrate on the frozen Banana River (*Nenana*, n.d.). The tradition has continued, although the pot is much higher, sometimes over $300,000. During the event, participants will try, between February and April, to guess the day and time the ice will break once winter has ended; the one who gets the closest earns the pot. The price for a ticket is $3.00 and can be purchased by those over 18 (*Nenana Ice Classic*, 2024).

DELTA JUNCTION: END OF THE ALASKA HIGHWAY

Delta Junction is located a short trip from Fairbanks, and although it is a small town with a little over 1,000 residents, there is a lot to see and do. Due to its agricultural presence, one of the main attractions is the fresh food served and sold in the local farmers market. Visitors can purchase fresh vegetables, different kinds of local meat, and other home-made products such as jams and baked goods.

While visiting downtown, it is possible to see several build-ings that are part of the town's history, such as the Sullivan Roadhouse, the oldest one in the state's Interior. The building was built in 1905 and is located at the end of the Alaska Highway. During the summer, its front garden is decorated with beautifully colored flowers, bringing life to the snow-covered structure during the other seasons of the year. Today, it serves as the local museum that preserves part of the town's history, including some of the original furni-ture and decorations used.

Another of the town's attractions is Rika's Roadhouse, the Big Delta State Historical Park's center building. It used to be an accommodation for visitors visiting the area and has been remodeled through time. However, it still maintains some of its original characteristics. As you enter the building, it is possible to see "part of the original kerosene crate floor [that] has been restored. The bedroom and kitchen are furnished in the 1920s and 1930s style. Furnishings were donated by local residents under the auspices of the Delta Historical Society" (*Visiting*, 2024).

Due to being settled on the banks of the Tanana River, water activities are very popular in the town. This includes fishing and kayaking, which can be done during warmer months when the river is not frozen. Its different green areas also offer hiking and trekking, wildlife observation, and other recreational activities for the whole family. Delta Junction and the surrounding area are home to five state parks, making it an ideal destination for those who want to engage in outdoor experiences.

FORT YUKON: ARCTIC VILLAGE EXPERIENCE

Located above the Arctic Circle, Fort Yukon is a short distance from Arctic Alaska and home to less than 600 inhabitants. Most of the people who live here are descendants of the Alaska Native people of Gwich'in, who still speak their native language and dialects. The town was an important trade post during the fur trade, whaling expansion, and the Klondike Gold Rush, serving as a settlement for many people who came to explore the area.

The town's name comes from being built on the margins of the Yukon River. However, visitors will need to catch a plane from Fairbanks to reach the region since the roads are blocked by snow most of the year. During the summer, it is possible to arrive by boat and stop to visit the smaller communities that survive on the river's margins.

Although the town is small, it is the perfect base for those who want to visit the Arctic part of Alaska. Several tour companies make the town their starting point for those visiting the extreme region. In addition to this, the town is also a short distance from national parks and wilderness areas. For those who intend to stay in the region, you find different water activities during the warmer months of the year. Keep in mind, though, that temperatures are usually below 0 °F during the winter.

Author's tip: If you are visiting Fort Yukon or expanding your trip further north, bringing everything you need is essential. Although the town has a grocery store where you can restock, a post office, and a health center, these services are otherwise limited. Chances are pretty good that you will not find what you are looking for. Therefore, preparing well and having all the essentials with you is better when going to the region.

TOK: GATEWAY TO ALASKA'S INTERIOR

If you are driving North from Canada through the Alaska Highway, Tok is the first town you will visit once you cross the border. One of the must-see places is the visitor center at the town's entrance. It is inside a massive timber building with all the information you need for your trip. There, you can find maps, tips, and brochures that will help guide you throughout your trip, regardless of the state region you want to visit.

Although initially established as a trading post, today it is considered a paradise for outdoor adventure enthusiasts. It has different recreational parks and a river where you can set up camp. The first of these parks is the Tok River State Recreation Site, which contains "27 campsites, six of which will accommodate motorhomes up to 60 feet in length. Facilities include a picnic shelter, drinking water, a walking trail, telephone, and latrines" (*Tok River State,* 2024).

Other recreational areas for visitors include the Moon Lake State Recreation Site and the Eagle Trail State Recreation Site, located approximately 15 miles from Tok and offering multiple campsites for outdoor adventures. These recreational areas include picnic sites, opportunities to observe wildlife, hiking trails, and even boat adventures near the water. Visitors can drive through the Tok Cut-Off Highway or the Alaska Highway to access these areas.

For those venturing into town, there are several accommodation and dining options.

ACCOMMODATION AND DINING

Although the towns in Interior Alaska are smaller than the other cities in the state, they offer visitors excellent accommodation and dining options. Lodging ranges from different campsites to resorts and more modest accommodations, and the cuisine in the region is very diversified. There are plenty of budget-friendly options and fancier places, depending on your desired experience. Read on to learn more about your choices to help you plan your stay in the area.

Accommodation

As you start looking for accommodation options, here are a few of the ones you might want to consider and where they are located:

- A Hyde Away B&B (Tok): $
- Alaska Frontier Inn (Delta Junction): $
- Chena Hot Springs Resort (Fairbanks): $$$
- Denali Princess Wilderness Lodge (Denali National Park): $$
- Fairbanks Princess Riverside Lodge (Fairbanks): $$

- Golden North Inn (Nenana): $$
- Hotel North Pole (North Pole): $$
- Pike's Waterfront Lodge (Fairbanks): $$
- Trophy Lodge (Delta Junction): $$
- Wedgewood Resort (Fairbanks): $$$

Dining

Here are some dining options to consider when visiting Interior Alaska. From a restaurant specializing in sausages made with different meat to a Michelin-starred Russian venue, you will certainly enjoy what the region offers.

Big Delta Brewing Company; Delta Junction; $$; Pizza

Chena's Alaskan Grill; Fairbanks; $$$; Grill and Alaskan

Chowder House; Fairbanks; $$; Seafood and sandwiches

Delta Meat and Sausage Co; Delta Junction; $$; Sausages made from different meats

Fast Eddy's Restaurant; Tok; $$; American

Geraldo's Restaurant; Fairbanks; $$; Italian

Jazz Bistro; Fairbanks; $$$; Latin and Spanish

Latitude 65; Fairbanks; $$$; American, Seafood

LaValle's Bistro; Fairbanks; $$, American and French

Prospector's Pizzeria; Denali National Park; $$; Pizza

Roughwoods Inn & Cafe; Nenana; $$; American and vegetarian

Soba; Fairbanks; $$; Russian

Sourdough Campground and Restaurant; Tok; $; American and cafe

Spicy Thai; North Pole; $$; Thai and Asian

The Pump House Restaurant & Saloon; Fairbanks; $$; American and grill

Turtle Club; Fox (just north of Fairbanks); $$$; American

Two Rivers Lodge; North Pole; $$$; American

As we move on to the final chapter of this book, it is time to explore the last region of Alaska. When learning about Far North Alaska, you will see how important the community is and how these Alaska Natives keep up their traditions. In what is close to one of the coldest regions on the planet, you will see much to explore in this area, including two national parks with landscapes that remain almost completely untouched. If you are ready for the final step of this adventure, read on!

FAR NORTH ALASKA

> *If you've never seen Alaska and experienced it for yourself, you just can't imagine what it's like—its pristine beauty and untamed wilderness will simply take your breath away!*

— SARAH PALIN

Alaska is a land of many wonders—beautiful landscapes, numerous wildlife, and a rich cultural heritage. The same can be said for the state's northernmost region and the U.S., Arctic Alaska. Contrary to what many may think, the region is populated by Alaska Natives and animals alike, offering the visitor the unique opportunity of seeing a landscape where the ice encounters the seawater and the forests, making it a unique opportunity for the breathtaking pictures.

In this last chapter, you will embark on an Arctic adventure beginning in Barrow, the northernmost city in the U.S. You will learn about the rich Inupiaq culture and witness the mesmerizing midnight sun during summer. Finally, you will learn about all the opportunities to explore the Arctic Coastal Plain and the significance of the end line of the Trans-Alaska Pipeline.

ARCTIC CIRCLE: CROSSING THE LINE INTO THE ARCTIC

The Arctic Circle is one of the most mystical places on Earth —and one of the coldest. Globally known as the home for polar bears and varied marine species, it remains one of the areas in the world that still has little to no human influence. The Arctic Circle has a circumference of approximately 9,900 square miles and is primarily covered by ice and snow. Although many people think that the Arctic is equivalent to the North Pole region, it, in fact, covers a much larger region: Northern Alaska.

According to *Frequently Asked Questions About the Arctic* (n.d.),

Unlike the Antarctic, the Arctic is inhabited by humans, including diverse Native communities with a longer history than many of the southerly societies. Although European-derived culture is now dominant in the Arctic, the study of the Native culture is important for its preservation and for what it can teach others about long-term human survival in the Arctic. The Arctic has many natural resources that could be developed for economic benefit. Crude oil, gold, industrial metals, and diamonds are presently being extracted, yet much of the Arctic's potential for natural resources is unknown. (Question 4)

The part of Alaska located in the Arctic Circle is mostly populated by Alaska Natives from the Iñupiat community, although there are also members from other Eskimo tribes. Their traditions, culture, and language continue to be present in the region, leading to the modification of the towns' names, as you will see. For those interested in discovering the majestic and incredible yet challenging experience that only the far north of Alaska can offer, read on.

KOTZEBUE: GATEWAY TO THE ARCTIC

With approximately 3,000 inhabitants, this town is the central hub for Arctic Alaska, of which almost 70% are Alaska Natives from the Iñupiat Eskimo community (*About Us*, 2024). Locally, it is known as Kikiktagruk, and as the largest town in the community, it supplies the 10 other nearby villages. However, much like the remainder of the region, prices tend to be higher than in other regions due to the difficulty of getting supplies.

Kotzebue is bathed by the sea and offers access to several different rivers, where fishing and other water recreational activities can be carried out. In the town, visitors will be able to find different lodging and dining locations. Some of the services in the area include restaurants, hotels, coffee shops, a grocery store, and a pharmacy. It is also where the main airport of the region, Kotzebue Airport, is located, and it has regular flights from other regions of the state.

However, despite all the local and natural beauty surrounding the Kotzebue region, the area's main attraction is the Kobuk Valley National Park. A curious characteristic of the park is that it has hundreds of miles of sand dunes and an unusual landscape for such a cold region. This is possible because, despite the freezing temperatures in the winter, the summer offers a mild climate, which can sometimes even be moderately warm. In this environment, animals such as caribou, birds, bears, ducks, salmon, and many others thrive without human interference.

Reaching the park can be challenging during some seasons of the year. Summer access is by plane, boat, or by foot. While it is possible to backpack from the Dalton Highway, through Gates of the Arctic National Park into Kobuk Valley National Park, it is logistically challenging and would take weeks (National Park Service, 2024b). The park has no roads or campgrounds, so camping is unadvised for inexperienced travelers. Backcountry camping is allowed for those who wish to do so. Those interested in spending time in the park will need to bring their own supplies, which can be bought in Kotzebue, 99 miles away.

UTQIAĠVIK (BARROW): THE NORTHERNMOST CITY IN THE UNITED STATES

This town that was once named Barrow has been the home of the Iñupiat Alaska Native community for the past 1,500 years, and their traditions continue to flourish. Visitors can learn about their traditions, language, and artifacts at the Iñupiat Heritage Center, also known as the Rooftop of the World. One of the major activities highlighted is whaling, which has been a part of the local tradition for centuries and continues to be a part of their subsistence.

The town is so remote that it is only accessible by plane or boat. While arriving there might be challenging, the reward for braving the region's fierce weather is the possibility of photographing several wildlife species that live in the area, including polar bears and wolves. Since visitors here will be on the margin of the Arctic Ocean, there is also the possibility of watching whales and other marine animals that inhabit the region, especially during the warmer months of the year.

One of the town's main characteristics is the amount of daylight it receives during the different seasons. In the summer, visitors can experience the "midnight sun," when there is sunlight throughout the whole day. On the other hand, during the winter, the opposite is possible, with the "polar night," when there is absolutely no sunlight for approximately 60 days.

Author's tip: To celebrate your arrival to one of the most unique places on Earth, look for the whalebone arch, which is located near the shore. There, you can take a picture under an arch made of a whale's jaw bones next to other objects made from the elements. It is certainly a picture-perfect opportunity that you do not want to miss!

PRUDHOE BAY: THE OILFIELDS AND ARCTIC COASTAL BEAUTY

Prudhoe Bay became an important center when oil was discovered in Alaska in the late 1960s. With this discovery, the government decided to build the Trans-Alaska Pipeline, which you have already read about in previous chapters. This pipeline extends 800 miles from the state's far north to the port of Valdez, in Prince William Sound. Although there is a highway connecting the bay to the remaining part of the state, the Dalton Highway, most people travel to the region and the small town of Deadhorse by plane. During the winter, with the heavy snow and ice, the driving conditions can be challenging and dangerous for those who are unfamiliar with driving in this weather.

Along with most other cities in the Arctic Circle, Prudhoe Bay experiences the midnight sun phenomenon and the polar night every year, lasting an average of 60 days. Although almost 500 miles away from Fairbanks, many choose to leave the central city in Interior Alaska for the adventure by car, where it will be possible to see amazing landscapes, encounter wildlife, and cross the Arctic Circle border until Deadhorse. This is the closest many people will get to Prudhoe Bay since access to the region where the pipeline starts is restricted for security reasons.

Different wildlife in the region that you might have a chance to see include grizzly, black, and polar bears, as well as caribou, sheep, and wolves. Despite being kept untouched for centuries, the discovery of new oil fields in the region has been attracting companies that are asking the American government to allow drilling in the area. This remains a conflict between those who want to drill and those who believe that drilling will negatively affect the region's ecosystems. The matter is still being debated by politicians.

Today, the construction of the Trans-Alaska pipeline has been responsible for most of the region's development, with many arriving to work in the area. This led to an increase in inhabitants in the nearby towns and others near one of the twelve pumping stations. While constructing the pipeline, engineers worked with the government and conservation specialists to design it for optimal oil transportation without disturbing wildlife. Tours to the oil drilling structure are available from Deadhorse by helicopter and plane, with starting prices at $250 per person.

ARCTIC NATIONAL WILDLIFE REFUGE: PRISTINE WILDERNESS

While visiting the Arctic region, seeing the wildlife species there is almost a must. There are few places on Earth where it is possible to see such an incredible area without human interference. Experiencing this untouched area and being able to see these animals up close is a unique experience that few are able to enjoy. Although it is possible to kayak and fish in the region, other outdoor activities, such as hiking and camping, are not recommended for inexperienced visitors because the lack of trails and designated areas makes it dangerous.

Today, the Arctic National Wild Refuge covers an area of 19 million acres and can only be accessed by plane. For those visiting for the first time, it is recommended to go on a guided tour with a knowledgeable professional familiar with the area. By joining one, you will have a greater chance of observing the bears, caribou, wolverines, and wolves on land and whales, walruses, and seals in the water.

While in the refuge, you can also visit the village of Kaktovik, where approximately 250 Alaska Natives from the Inupiaq community live and receive visitors who want to see polar bears. From there, it is possible to see the mountains, glaciers, and the sea with blue skies in the background, offering amazing picture opportunities. The refuge can be reached from different Alaskan cities, where an air service will take visitors to the region. The most popular tours depart from Deadhorse, Coldfoot, Fairbanks, Fort Yukon, and Kaktovik.

NOME: GOLD RUSH HISTORY AND IDITAROD FINISH LINE

Nome is famous for its status as the finish line for the Iditarod Trail Sled Dog Race that starts in Anchorage. After trailing over 935 miles of snow and open areas, it is here that the dog mushers arrive to a great festival that is held at their point of arrival, the Red Fox Olson Trail Monument. As each musher passes through the main street, the fire siren sounds, greeting those who arrive. On Sunday, after the race, the participants and the community have a banquet with awards and recognition prizes.

Despite its population of just under 4,000 people, Nome is one of the most popular destinations in Alaska, and the longer you stay, the more you will be able to see and explore. One of these is the area of Alaska's most famous gold rush site. It happened in the early 1900s and attracted thousands of people trying their luck to find the precious metal. Today, many of the structures from this time remain and can still be seen and visited by travelers who want to know more about the local history (DeVaughn et al., 2023).

While strolling downtown Nome, visitors can see different art galleries with crafts made by Alaska Natives and observe structures from the past when over 200,000 people lived in the region. There are also several lodging and dining opportunities and perfect places to take pictures and record their visit. To reach the town, you will need to catch a flight or boat since no roads are leading to it.

For outdoor sports enthusiasts, there are several activities to engage in as you visit the region. These include wildlife watching, sports and ice fishing, hiking, horseback riding, and skiing. Local tours can also be taken to flightseeing areas, including the Bering Land Bridge National Preserve tundra. With these tours, visitors can enjoy the region's incredible landscape and see some wildlife, including grizzly and polar bears, seals, walruses, caribou, and oxen. If you are looking for a mixed experience of urban areas and outdoors within the Arctic region, Nome is certainly the place to go!

POINT HOPE: HISTORIC ESKIMO VILLAGE

The final village of our journey could not be more special: Point Hope. This small town of just over 800 people is one of the oldest continuously occupied regions of the country where the Native Ipiutak Eskimos lived and created the famous igloos. Here, the community built homes partially under the land to protect their families from the cold and harsh weather during the winter. For subsistence, they hunted whales in the nearby sea, which was one of the ways to reach the village and is still used today. The other way is to fly in, as with many other Alaskan communities.

Today, with a predominant population of Alaska Natives, many of its inhabitants speak their dialects. One of the major festivals in the village happens during the summer when whaling crews gather to celebrate what they have caught in the Nalukataq festival (*Our Roots*, n.d.). Whaling and hunting are their main source of survival, characterizing it as a subsistence community with several resources to obtain their livelihood from. This is certainly one of the best places in Alaska to see how the traditional communities live and experience their culture.

Visitors to the village will be able to hear stories from the community's elders, watch ethnic dances, and eat some of the local food made with the products that are caught. Another highlight will be visiting prehistoric village sites and old burial grounds, one marked by large standing whale bones (*Point Hope*, n.d.). Today, the region suffers from erosion and floods, which have damaged many of its original constructions, causing the village to relocate in the 1970s to a higher and safer location.

Author's tip: Those interested in learning more about the community before visiting can watch the documentary *Point Hope, Alaska*, filmed in 2016. The movie discusses the history of whaling and the village's culture, showing the importance of their traditions and unity as time passes.

ACCOMMODATION AND DINING

Although the Arctic part of Alaska is a more remote region, this does not mean that it doesn't have the structure to receive visitors to the area to explore. In fact, those who go to this region will see that there is a great variety of accommodations and dining options to choose from. However, it is important to remember that due to its more remote location, the prices are higher than other areas due to the difficulty in obtaining supplies.

Accommodation

The major lodging options in Arctic Alaska are in Utqiaġvik, Kotzebue, and Nome, the largest cities in the region. However, you will find that the prices may not be as budget-friendly as in other cities and towns with more options. On the positive side, by staying in these properties, you will be helping the local economy and the Natives of the region, many of whom depend on the annual tourist influx to generate income. Here are some of the options you might want to consider when visiting the area:

- Angel Camp by the Sea (Nome): $$
- Arctic Getaway B&B (Wiseman): $$
- Aurora Inn and Executive Suites (Nome): $$
- Aurora Pointe Activity Center (Utqiaġvik): $$
- Bettles Lodge (Bettles): $$
- Boreal Lodge (Coldfoot): $$
- Coldfoot Camp (Coldfoot): $
- Dredge No.7 Inn (Nome): $$
- King Eider Inn of Barrow Alaska (Utqiaġvik): $$$

- Lagoon Bed and Breakfast (Kotzebue): $$
- Northern Inn (Point Hope): $$
- Nullagvik Hotel (Kotzebue): $$$
- Sunny Willow (Kotzebue): $$
- Top of the World Hotel (Utqiaġvik): $$$
- Tundra Rose Cabins (Wiseman): $$$

If you plan camping, you must bring the necessary supplies, including very warm clothes and canned food (and a can opener!). The major cities to stock up are the largest in the region, Utqiaġvik, Nome, and Kotzebue. These towns are the best places to find different supply options. They will also be the ideal places to establish a basecamp should you need to come back and let others know where you are going.

Dining

Similar to lodging, restaurants in the Alaskan Arctic region are not as fancy as restaurants in other regions of the state. However, this does not mean that the food isn't as good. In fact, many people are surprised by the delicious taste of the local cuisine and the variety it presents. When visiting, you will find many restaurants that serve pizza and traditional American food, as well as the occasional Asian and Mexican restaurants. However, when in the region, you will really want to try the local baked and cooked delicacies, which can warm your body even on the coldest days.

Arctic Pizza; Utqiaġvik; $; Pizza

Arctic Slice; Point Hope; $$; Pizza

Board of Trade Saloon; Nome; $; American

Coldfoot Camp; Coldfoot; $$; American

Cruz's Mexican Grill; Utqiaġvik; $$; Mexican

Empress Chinese Restaurant; Kotzebue; $$; Chinese

Niggivikput; Utqiaġvik; $$$; American

Northern Lights Restaurant; Utqiaġvik; $$$; Asian

Nullagvik Restaurant; Kotzebue; $$; American

Osaka Restaurant; Utqiaġvik; $$; Japanese

Pingo Bakery; Nome; $$; Seafood

Polar Café; Nome; $$; American

Sam & Lee's Restaurant; Utqiaġvik; $$; Chinese

Uutuku; Kotzebue; $; Asian

You now have information on everything you must know about Alaska and everything you must consider as you plan your visit. We have explored all its different regions, attractions, and characteristics, making choosing the adventure you want to embark on easier. As we wrap up your journey, I invite you to embark on one last quest before you start planning and preparing. Are you ready for your next vacation?

CONCLUSION

Alaska is the perfect destination for an unforgettable vacation filled with incredible adventures because it offers everyone an experience that they will not soon forget. Do you want to see wildlife and explore nature? You can certainly do it in one of its many national parks. If you prefer an urban setting, Anchorage, Juneau, and Fairbanks are for you. Those who prefer water sports will find plenty of opportunities to do so, as will those who would rather hike, mountaineer, and ski.

The wildlife in the state is often one of the most attractive features for visitors. Where else in nature can you find all three types of bears? Where else can you fish for all five types of salmon and taste them in delicious dishes of various cuisines? These are just a couple of the many elements that Alaska has to offer, considering its ecological adventures.

At the same time, for those looking to learn more about history and Alaska Native culture and traditions, there are many opportunities to do so. As you travel through the different communities, it is possible to learn about all the Native communities still inhabit the state and are so present in its daily life. Whether you are speaking to the elders, visiting museums, participating in events, or admiring the local art, it is possible to see all the rich traditions still kept by its people.

Remember to write down all the safety elements that we discussed, which need to be considered for your trip if you are venturing out on your own. Preparation will be key to ensure that you have a good experience. Even if you are traveling some time from now, use this opportunity to start booking the hotels where you want to stay and signing up for the tours you are interested in. Doing this in advance means avoiding higher prices, finding the best deals for your trip, and ensuring you can do everything you want.

Alaska, the last frontier, is certainly where you will find the best of all worlds, regardless of what you seek. Good food, attractions, festivals, outdoor activities, friendly locals, history, nature, and lots of excitement and adventure. Will you miss the opportunity to travel to one of the most exciting and unexplored places on Earth? I hope not! Visiting Alaska will offer you everything that you have read about and even more. It is certainly an experience you cannot miss.

Now, it is your turn to take the next step. You now have all the information you need to dive into the planning process, choose your adventure, and set the wheels—or wings—in motion. Alaska's untamed beauty, rich culture, and unparalleled wilderness are calling. From the towering peaks of Denali to the serene waters of Glacier Bay, every corner of this majestic state has a story to tell. Safe travels, and enjoy your trip!

Thank you for choosing to read this book, and I wish you all the best as you plan your trip to Alaska. If you feel this book has helped you plan your next vacation and has helped you to better understand each of Alaska's regions, please leave a review,

Reviews from readers like you support independent writers!

REFERENCES

About us. (2024). City of Kotzebue. https://www.cityofkotzebue.-com/index.asp?Type=B_BASIC&SEC=

Alaska bush aircraft. (n.d.). Alaska Outdoors Supersite. https://alaskaout-doorssupersite.com/activities/flying

Alaska Department of Fish and Game. (2024). *Alaska's species information.* https://www.adfg.alaska.gov/index.cfm?adfg=species.main

Alaska Dog Mushers Association. (2024). *Open North American Championships.* https://alaskadogmushers.com/open-north-american-championships/

Alaska fairs & festivals. (2024). Alaska.org. https://www.alaska.org/things-to-do/festivals

Alaska Kids' Corner. (n.d.). State of Alaska. https://alaska.gov/kids/student.htm

Alaska native culture. (n.d.). Travel Alaska. https://www.travelalaska.-com/Things-To-Do/Alaska-Native-Culture

Alaska Native festivals & events. (2024). Travel Alaska. https://www.travelalas-ka.com/Things-To-Do/Alaska-Native-Culture/Alaska-Native-Festivals-Events

Alaska Native Heritage Center. (n.d.). Alaska.org. https://www.alaska.org/de-tail/alaska-native-heritage-center

Alaska RV, Motorhome & Campervan Rental. (n.d.). Alaska.org. https://www.alaska.org/transportation/rv-rental

Alaska's history and culture. (n.d.). Alaska Cruises. https://www.alaskacruises.-com/cruises/history-and-culture.html

Aleutian Islands Wilderness. (2018). Wilderness.net. https://wilder-ness.net/visit-wilderness/?ID=5

Angela. (2022, September 12). *Driving in Alaska: Everything You Need to Know.* Global Gadding. https://www.globalgadding.com/driving-in-alaska/

Annie. (2020, April 8). *Flying to Alaska: How to get the best deal on airfares.* Alaska Tours. https://alaskatours.com/alaska-stories/flying-to-alaska-how-to-get-the-best-deal-on-airfares/

Arts & traditions. (n.d.). Travel Alaska. https://www.travelalaska.com/Things-To-Do/Alaska-Native-Culture/Arts-Traditions

Bear viewing in Alaska. (2024). Travel Alaska. https://www.travelalaska.-com/Things-To-Do/Wildlife-Viewing/Bear-Viewing

REFERENCES

Butcher, S. (2024). Iditarod Trail Sled Dog Race. In *Encyclopædia Britannica*. https://www.britannica.com/sports/Iditarod-Trail-Sled-Dog-Race

Community. (n.d.). North Pole Alaska. https://www.northpolealaska.com/community/

DeVaughn, M., Galesa, C., Ellanna, L., Knowlton, K., & Trujillo, M. (2023). *There is no place like Nome*. Nome Chamber of Commerce. https://assets.website-files.com/5b7f1dde7a3a9c59566e2f86/63f7d72850631f0cd-c827ca1_nome_guide_2023.pdf

Dillingham. (n.d.). Travel Alaska. https://www.travelalaska.com/Destinations/Cities-Towns/Dillingham

Fairbanks. (n.d.). Travel Alaska. https://www.travelalaska.com/Destinations/Cities-Towns/Fairbanks

5 reasons why Alaska should be on your travel list. (2023, March 9). Regent Seven Seas Cruises. https://www.rssc.com/discover-more/blog/5-reasons-why-alaska-should-be-on-your-travel-list

Frequently asked questions about the Arctic. (n.d.). National Oceanic and Atmospheric Administration. https://www.pmel.noaa.gov/arctic-zone/faq.html

Getting to & around Alaska by ferry. (n.d.). Travel Alaska. https://www.travelalaska.com/Getting-To-Around/By-Ferry

Getting to & around Alaska: Drive. (n.d.). Travel Alaska. https://www.travelalaska.com/Getting-To-Around/Drive

Getting to & around Alaska: Fly. (n.d.). Travel Alaska. https://www.travelalaska.com/getting-to-around/fly

Ghangas, S. (2022, January 3). *12 vibrant festivals in Alaska: All about how the Alaskans celebrate!* Travel Triangle. https://traveltriangle.com/blog/festivals-in-alaska/

Gregg, E. (2023, October 12). *From glaciers to gold mines: the inside guide to Juneau, Alaska's capital city*. National Geographic. https://www.nationalgeographic.com/travel/article/paid-content-inside-guide-juneau-alaska

History.com. (2022, December 21). *Alaska*. https://www.history.com/topics/us-states/alaska

Iditarod - The Last Great Race. (2024). Iditarod. https://iditarod.com/#

Joseph, S. (2023, March 6). *101 inspirational alaska quotes, sayings & puns*. Learn about States. https://www.learnaboutstates.com/alaska/alaska-quotes-gp1/

Juneau. (n.d.). Travel Alaska. https://www.travelalaska.com/Destinations/Cities-Towns/Juneau

King Salmon. (n.d.). Travel Alaska. https://www.travelalaska.com/Destinations/Cities-Towns/King-Salmon

Kodiak Island. (n.d.). Alaska Department of Fish and Game. https://www.ad-fg.alaska.gov/index.cfm?adfg=viewinglocations.kodiak

Lynch, D., & Miller, M. M. (2019). History of Alaska. In *Encyclopædia Britannica*. https://www.britannica.com/place/Alaska/History

Maloney, L. (2023, September 24). *Traveling by bush plane in Alaska*. Moon Travel Guides. https://www.moon.com/travel/planning/traveling-by-bush-plane-in-alaska/

Meeuwesen, J. (2020, January 26). *15 best things to do in Bethel (Alaska)*. The Crazy Tourist. https://www.thecrazytourist.com/15-best-things-to-do-in-bethel-alaska/

National Park Service. (2021, September 5). *Traditional knowledge*. United States National Park Service. https://www.nps.gov/locations/alaska/traditional-knowledge.htm

National Park Service. (2022). *"Voices of Glacier Bay" soundscape project*. United States National Park Service. https://www.nps.gov/glba/learn/nature/soundscape.htm

National Park Service. (2023). *Katmai National Park & Preserve*. United States National Park Service. https://www.nps.gov/katm/index.htm

National Park Service. (2024a). *Wrangell-St Elias National Park & Preserve*. United States National Park Service. https://www.nps.gov/wrst/index.htm

National Park Service. (2024b, February 26). *Kobuk Valley National Park*. United States National Park Service. https://www.nps.gov/kova/planyourvisit/things2do.htm

Nation's #1 fishing port. (2024). Unalaska Visitor's Bureau. http://www.unalaska.org/nations-1-fishing-port.html

Nenana. (n.d.). Travel Alaska. https://www.travelalaska.com/Destinations/Cities-Towns/Nenana

Nenana Ice Classic. (2024). Nenana Ice Classic. https://www.nenanaakiceclassic.com/

North Pole. (n.d.). Travel Alaska. https://www.travelalaska.com/Destinations/Cities-Towns/North-Pole

Northern lights. (n.d.). Travel Alaska. https://www.travelalaska.com/Things-To-Do/Northern-Lights

Origin of names of US states. (n.d.). US Department of Interior Indian Affairs. https://www.bia.gov/as-ia/opa/online-press-release/origin-names-us-states

Our roots. (n.d.). Tikigaq. https://www.tikigaq.com/tikigaq-story

Petroglyph Beach State Historic Site. (n.d.). Alaska.org. https://www.alaska.org/detail/petroglyph-beach-state-historic-site

REFERENCES

Point Hope. (n.d.). Arctic Slope Native Association. https://arctic-slope.org/about/communities/point-hope/

Prince William Sound. (n.d.). Alaska Department of Fish and Game. https://www.adfg.alaska.gov/index.cfm?adfg=viewinglocations.pws

Risk Management Team. (2003). *Remote travel safety guide.* University of Alaska. https://www.alaska.edu/risksafety/download/RemoteTravelSafetyGuide.pdf

Silverstein, E. (2023, July 9). *Alaska cruise guide: Best itineraries, planning tips and things to do.* The Points Guy. https://thepointsguy.com/guide/alaska-cruise-guide/

Sitka Sound Science Center. (n.d.). Alaska.org. https://www.alaska.org/detail/sitka-sound-science-center

Stabinska, A. (2023, October 31). *Bear viewing in Alaska - best places, tours & tips.* Alaska Itinerary. https://alaskaitinerary.com/bear-viewing-alaska/

Tok River State Recreation Site. (2024). Alaska Department of Natural Resources. https://dnr.alaska.gov/parks/aspunits/northern/tokrvsrs.htm

Top 5 fishing destinations in Alaska. (2017). Alaska Tour Jobs. https://www.alaskatourjobs.com/blog/outdoor-activities/top-5-fishing-destinations-alaska/

Totem Heritage Center. (n.d.). Experience Ketchikan. https://www.experienceketchikan.com/totem-heritage-center.html

Travel Alaska. (2024, January). *Alaska Native Culture.* https://digital.milespartnership.com/publication/?m=68361&i=803835&p=2&ver=html5

Unalaska. (n.d.). Alaska.org. https://www.alaska.org/destination/dutch-harbor-unalaska

The Valley of 10,000 Smokes. (n.d.). Alaska.org. https://www.alaska.org/detail/the-valley-of-ten-thousand-smokes

Visiting. (2024). Delta Junction. https://deltajunction.us/visiting-delta-junction/

What to Do on a Ferry: 12 useful tips. (2021, July 9). Ferry Hopper. https://www.ferryhopper.com/en/blog/stories/what-to-do-on-board

When traveling. (n.d.). Alaska Railroad. https://www.alaskarailroad.com/travel-planning/when-traveling

White Pass & Yukon Route Railroad. (n.d.). Alaska.org. https://www.alaska.org/detail/white-pass-yukon-route-railroad

Wildlife in Alaska. (2022, February 15). U.S. National Park Service. https://www.nps.gov/subjects/aknatureandscience/akwildlife.htm

IMAGE REFERENCES

BarbaraJackson. (2014, November 9). *Alaska fishing salmon kasilof.* Pixabay. https://pixabay.com/photos/alaska-fishing-salmon-kasilof-524529/

Beugels, J. (2019, January 23). *Into the wilderness.* Unsplash. https://unsplash.-com/photos/winding-road-under-blue-sky-L8bZAwmQK1M

Brad. (2019, December 29). Body of water and mountains during day. In *Unsplash.* https://unsplash.com/photos/body-of-water-and-mountains-during-day-tQksclxDyWY

Buonemani, J. (2017, September 9). *Come fly with me.* Unsplash. https://unsplash.com/photos/red-and-white-rusts-n46612-biplane-on-body-of-water-Y9N5KCkPGNU

Cornelissen, T. (2019, July 31). *People walking on wooden dock.* Pexels. https://www.pexels.com/photo/people-walking-on-wooden-dock-12761922/

Dan, C. (2019, August 15). *White street signgages.* Unsplash. https://unsplash.-com/photos/white-street-signgages-znT9lFjTgFg

Howard, M. (2015, November 11). *Calm lake water near snowy mountain peak under cloudy skies.* Unsplash. https://unsplash.com/photos/calm-lake-water-near-snowy-mountain-peak-under-cloudy-skies-gjD66bFxpKE

Keil, J. (2019, May 18). *White and black toy train on track selective focus photography.* Unsplash. https://unsplash.com/photos/white-and-black-toy-train-on-track-selective-focus-photography-V9j3e5Dtvso

Likesilkto. (2015, Nevermber 23). *Aurora Alaska Fairbanks snow sky.* Pixabay. https://pixabay.com/photos/aurora-alaska-fairbanks-snow-sky-1057948/

Long, R. (2022, August 16). *A group of seals lying on a rock.* Unsplash. https://unsplash.com/photos/a-group-of-seals-lying-on-a-rock-MZ0m9XRO06s

Mager, H.-J. (2020, June 6). *Polar bear on snow covered ground during daytime.* Unsplash. https://unsplash.com/photos/polar-bear-on-snow-covered-ground-during-daytime-CHqbiMhQ_wE

Nandakumar, H. (2018, July 17). *Mountain and blue body of water under cloudy sky.* Unsplash. https://unsplash.com/photos/mountain-and-blue-body-of-water-under-cloudy-sky-eANcXwBWzSw

Nayak, P. (2021, October 14). *Mother teaches her cubs how to fish from the lip of Brook's Falls for upstream Salmon. The cubs patiently watch their mother and learn.* Unsplash. https://unsplash.com/photos/a-group-of-brown-bears-standing-on-top-of-a-waterfall-21fFzg-8MM8

REFERENCES

Pixabay. (2016, January 16). *Mountain filled with snow near calm sea under white clouds and blue sky during daytime.* Pexels. https://www.pexels.com/photo/mountain-filled-with-snow-near-calm-sea-under-white-clouds-and-blue-sky-during-daytime-35637/

PublicDomainPictures. (2012, March 1). *Totem pole faces Alaska American.* Pixabay. https://pixabay.com/photos/totem-pole-faces-alaska-american-21040/

Robzor. (2015, March 11). *Train Alaska travel railway.* Pixabay. https://pixabay.com/photos/train-alaska-travel-railway-668964/

Shankar, D. (2022, September 28). A body of water with trees and mountains in the background. In *Unsplash.* https://unsplash.com/photos/a-body-of-water-with-trees-and-mountains-in-the-background-GaqYlwPFno8

Tan, B. (2019, December 24). *People riding sled on snow covered ground.* Pexels. https://www.pexels.com/photo/people-riding-sled-on-snow-covered-ground-5389771/

Venkataraman, S. (2023, September 15). *A brown bear wading through a body of water.* Unsplash. https://unsplash.com/photos/a-brown-bear-wading-through-a-body-of-water-TcudCwgE59w

Vizek, J. (2021, June 23). *Snow covered mountain during daytime.* Unsplash. https://unsplash.com/photos/snow-covered-mountain-during-daytime-qH70Bp7mjyU

Made in the USA
Monee, IL
28 May 2024

59058941R00100